THE HEART OF THE DIACONATE

THE
HEART
OF THE
DIACONATE

COMMUNION WITH THE
SERVANT MYSTERIES
OF CHRIST

JAMES KEATING

Paulist Press
New York / Mahwah, NJ

The section in Chapter 2 "The Sacred Character of Holy Orders" pages 43–52 was previously published as "The Character of Diaconal Ordination" in *Ignatius Insight*, August 17, 2010. Used with permission.

The section in Chapter 2 "The Principles of Ministry" pages 38–42 was previously published as "The Moral Life: The Spiritual Poverty of the Diaconate" in *Church Life: Catholic Education and the New Evangelization*, vol. 2, no. 2 (September 20, 2013) pages 1–4. Used with permission.

Cover design by Susan Webb
Book design by Lynn Else

Library of Congress Cataloging-in-Publication Data

Keating, James.
    The heart of the diaconate : communion with the servant mysteries of Christ / James Keating.
        pages cm
    ISBN 978-0-8091-4917-9 (pbk. : alk. paper) — ISBN 978-1-58768-480-7 (ebook)
    1. Deacons—Catholic Church. I. Title.
    BX1912.K26 2015
    262'.142—dc23

                                                                2014035540

ISBN 978-0-8091-4917-9 (paperback)
ISBN 978-1-58768-480-7 (e-book)

Published by Paulist Press
997 Macarthur Boulevard
Mahwah, New Jersey 07430

www.paulistpress.com

Printed and bound in the
United States of America

Dedication
Deacon Robert Jergovic (1954–2011)

In Gratitude to
Archbishop George Lucas for his commitment to the renewal
of diaconal formation in the Archdiocese of Omaha

CONTENTS

FOREWORD

Deacon James Keating has delivered a timely and significant reflection on the nature of the diaconate and its importance in the Church's mission.

The first deacon ordinations are recorded in the Acts of the Apostles, where the apostles are shown praying and laying hands on seven candidates, described as "seven men of good standing, full of the Spirit and of wisdom" (Acts 6:3). In that initial deacon class was St. Stephen, a great defender of the faith and the first Christian martyr. Another of the seven was St. Philip, a father of four who was known as "the evangelist." He was a key figure in the Church's early mission to the Gentiles, and is remembered for his dramatic baptism of the Ethiopian queen's attendant.

Permanent deacons today still play a vital role in the Church's mission of evangelization. Here in Los Angeles, the nation's largest archdiocese, we have nearly four hundred permanent deacons serving in parishes, schools, and a diverse array of ministries and leadership positions. In their service of love to the family of God, deacons are essential co-workers in my ministry as Archbishop.

As Deacon Keating discusses, the ministry of the permanent deacon is far more than "functional." The deacon is neither a glorified layman nor a "junior priest." In the mystery of God's saving plan, the deacon is called to minister *in persona Christi Servi*—in the person of Christ the Servant. He is configured to a deep identification with Christ, his sacred character and identity conferred by the apostles' successors, the bishops, in the sacrament of Holy Orders.

"Whoever serves me must follow me," Jesus said, "and where I am, there will my servant be also" (John 12:26). The deacon walks with Jesus Christ in imitation of his ministry of love and service. Ordination configures him to Jesus in his most humble form—as the Son of God who emptied himself to come among us in the form of a servant; as the Son of Man who came not to be served, but to serve.

Deacon Keating speaks of the "creative tension" in the deacon's identity. The deacon is, he says, a man with a foot in both worlds, "a cleric living a lay life."

In the early Church, the deacon is decisively distinguished from the priest. This is true especially in the liturgy, where he assisted the bishop and priest but never himself celebrated the Eucharist. However, from the beginning, the deacon was always understood to be a cleric. The words of the *Catechism* on this point are striking. The deacon, by ordination, is given the sacramental character of "Christ, who made himself the 'deacon' or servant of all."[1] The deacon's vocation of service is thus profoundly *ecclesial*. He is ordained to serve the Church, in the hierarchy of service that Christ intended for his Church.

Deacons are servants of the bishop in his service of the people of God. The *Apostolic Constitutions*, an early Church manual, calls the deacon, "the angel and the prophet of the

---

1. *Catechism of the Catholic Church*, 2nd ed., Washington, DC: United States Catholic Conference, 1997), no. 1570. Cf. Mk 10:45; Lk 22:27; St. Polycarp, *Ad Phil.* 5,2:SCh 10,182.

bishop." From the beginning, the bishop and his deacons have been united in a sacred bond—in their ministry of service and their testimony to their faith, and often in the history of the Church, in the ultimate witness they offer, the witness of their lives. Especially in the first Christian centuries, the Church's bishops were often martyred alongside their deacons.

Deacon Keating attests that we are living in a new time of mission for the Church in the Americas, what recent popes have been calling the time of the "continental mission" and the "new evangelization." Furthermore, he understands that in order to serve this mission, today's deacons need not only doctrinal, moral, and pastoral formation. Today's deacons also require a rich interior life of prayer, a deep desire to live in the heart of Christ, and a passion to share his gospel of mercy and love. He reminds us that the heart of Jesus Christ must be the heart of the deacon's life and ministry.

In the ancient liturgies, the deacon was given the task of dismissing the faithful at the conclusion of the Mass. He was the one who pronounced the words, *"Ite, missa est."* This remains a powerful image of the possibilities for the diaconate in the Church's new evangelization. Ordained to serve both in the world and alongside the priest at the altar, the deacon is uniquely positioned to call us to live the mysteries we celebrate and also to witness to how we glorify God with our lives and serve our neighbors in love.

Deacon Keating's book offers us clear reflections and a sound path for the renewal of this ancient and vital ministry in the Church.

Most Reverend José H. Gomez
Archbishop of Los Angeles

INTRODUCTION
EVER NEW

As the fiftieth anniversary of the Diaconate in the United States approaches, it is appropriate to reflect upon its character and future role in a Church that is experiencing significant development in clerical formation. The diaconate exists as a vocation of creative tension—a cleric living a lay life—and must remain in this tension if the church is to possess, in any concrete way, a diaconal imagination. A future diaconate must be one that involves a deeper appropriation of the servant identity of Christ, an appropriation that ignites the public witness of deacons so as to attract younger men to this vocation and end what can only be called its "retirement" culture. The diaconate will find its way into the imagination of the church when those who respond to Christ's call not only want to "help out" around the parish but have also been encouraged by bishops to receive spiritual vision. The men who carry the diaconate into the future will be those who have *a deep interiority*, a ministry sustained by conscious *communion with the Trinity*, and an *enlivened* sense of evangelization. It will also entail a deepening encouragement by the leaders in diaconal formation to invite minority communities—both ethnic and racial—to see the diaconate as a viable vocation for young men with families. Holiness that flows from the diaconal identity of the church is not an endeavor for later in life; it is a summons from Christ that attracts all.

For the celibate deacon, it will be a life of uncommon service, one established in a creative appropriation of a singular dedication to God and church. Celibacy for the permanent deacon is embraced as a way of life further marking the Christic unity of Holy Orders, as the deacon shares in Christ's own celibate service to others. He offers his body to God, a body that now becomes a sign of Christ's own ministerial availability in both prayer and charity. More commonly, this availability, fundamentally nourished by sacramental participation, finds a place within the hearts of generous wives and husbands. The diaconal vocation can inhere in a man who *privileges* his marriage vows in such a *secure* way that these vows *can be taken up* into, but not be absorbed by, Christ's own servant mysteries.

Whether the vocation finds expression within the celibate life or marriage vows, the future of the diaconate is mystical, youthful, and possessing one evangelical question, "Where has the gospel yet to reach, and how may I announce it in those places?" This question has profound implications regarding future diaconal ministerial assignments and carries the potential to finally instill within the local church a diaconate that is truly diocesan and not simply parochial.

HOLY ORDERS

In the wider ecclesial culture, a deeper formational revolution must occur if the sacrament of Holy Orders is to have a more united and spiritually mature future. Seminary formation must include an intentional formation into the diaconate. This formation is crucial since *becoming a deacon is a prerequisite* to priesthood. Without such a revolution in seminary formation, there will continue to be an anemic diaconal imagination in many priests. This weak imagination is caused when seminarians reach beyond diaconal identity to priesthood *in a premature way*. There can be *no* sacrifice (priesthood) without service (diaconate). It was only through Christ's service, which flowed from his ongoing prayer of communion with the Father, that sacrifice became his established priestly identity upon Calvary. Without a diaconal imagination, the priest may be tempted to think that his presiding at the sacramental mysteries results from his embrace of celibacy or his acumen into theological studies. In fact, christologically, the priest's presence at Calvary is due only to his descent into the deepest points of human need, pain, and poverty. Christ, the high priest (see Heb 4:15), could only be "raised up" after he humbled himself to share in our humanity. The movement into priestly sacrifice flows through self-emptying love.

> Every priest, of course, *also continues as a deacon* and must always be aware of this dimension, for the Lord himself became our minister, our deacon. Recall the act of the washing of the feet, where it is explicitly shown that the Teacher, the Lord, acts as a deacon and wants those who follow him to be deacons and carry out this ministry for humanity, to the point that they even help us to wash the dirty feet of the people entrusted to our care. This dimension seems to me to be of paramount importance.[1]

One can only become a priest if one has first contemplated and embraced, in imperfect ways, the main awe-inspiring movement of God who became flesh: "Christ Jesus,

> who, though he was in the form of God,
>   did not regard equality with God
>   as something to be exploited,
> but emptied himself,
>   taking the form of a slave,
>   being born in human likeness."
>   (Phil 2:5–7)

Without *descent*, no man can *ascend* to the altar of sacrifice. To circumvent the descent into service by not fully appropriating it as the established foundation of priesthood is to plant the cross of priestly sacrifice upon sand. To further deepen the reverence due to the diaconal mysteries in priestly formation will not only bring the sacrament of Holy Orders into a new season of maturity but concord between the grades of orders.

Regarding the lower rank of Holy Orders, diaconal formation, there has to be new emphasis upon welcoming candidates that are interested in the spiritual life, the theological life, and the liturgical life. Since its reestablishment in the West, the permanent diaconate has rightly focused upon pastoral ministry but has suffered from inattention to a man's more profound appropriation of the Word, prayer, and contemplation. One cannot be ordained simply to "help out," for ordination is a *sacred* ministry, and the one so ordained has to be fascinated with the sacred and interested in contemplating it so as to better share its beauty in prayer with others, and to preach and teach with power. Pastoral ministry that does not originate in, nor is sustained by, interior intimacy with the servant mysteries of Christ is neither pastoral nor ministry, it is humanitarian aid. With both the needed revolution in diaconal seminary formation and a renewed discernment about the spiritual qualities one needs to be a deacon, a creative vibrancy will be unleashed in those who inhabit Holy Orders.

Notes

1. Benedict XVI, Meeting with the Clergy of the Diocese of Rome, February 7, 2008.

1

CALLING

DISCERNING THE CALL

In order to discern a call to the diaconate, a man must first listen to what he truly loves. He does this by paying attention to the fruit of his life. Does he have a real and deepening prayer life? Does he love the Catholic Church and participate in it as his primary community of identity eschewing any ideologically based sources of conscience formation? Does he have a marital life of intimate and trusting communication? Is he a father who guides his children's consciences? Does his work or professional life record a stable and competent history? Can he be a good friend to others? Do his actions reveal a desire to help those who carry emotional, spiritual, or economic wounds? The first question that is raised in diaconal discernment is what or whom do I love? To what or whom do I give my attention to the most? What we pay attention to, we become, and so the *human* formation of a man who is discerning diaconate is paramount in consideration before he can be welcomed into formation.

Holy Orders builds upon the foundation of human maturation and the measure of human maturation is Christ. Christ is the anthropological standard against which one can ascertain the presence of moral and spiritual character (see Eph 4:11–15). A deacon director and the diaconal inquirer himself have to look

5

to human character development when discerning God's call to Holy Orders. In diaconal ministry, competency in human skills and virtues such as communication, prudence, humility, and professional demeanor matter a great deal. People can judge deacons severely if their demeanor and competency are below standard. Since diaconal ministry is not "essential" in the sense that a priest is "needed" to hear confessions, celebrate Eucharist, and anoint the sick, the deacon can be easily dismissed if he doesn't possess a strong human foundation of moral character, education, and skill upon which he can build the ministry that Christ is sharing with him.

This human foundation establishes the man as either a bridge to Christ or an obstacle (Directory, 189). Since the pool of deacon candidates is usually quite large, a stricter discernment by the director and the bishop at the threshold of inquiry should be the norm. There needs to be a solid foundation upon which grace and the church can form a public minister. An unstable human foundation may well be enough to turn people away from a man who is supposed to be an invitatory evangelical presence. Unlike priestly formation programs where the candidates are younger and there is a well-founded hope that seminary living itself might move them from self-preoccupation to virtue, the diaconate attracts a "finished product" so to speak. For deacon directors, the human formation component in any inquirer is more urgent to consider because the permanent diaconate process, unlike seminary, does not have the luxury of time.

The people of the local church will ignore and spurn a man who remains emotionally immature or presents an unusual personality. Ordaining such men is unfair to the church and to the man, as his ministerial consolation will be minimal and his ministry may stall. The first step in discerning a diaconal vocation is the character of the man, the human substance that sits before the deacon director and is not fully known in his readied expressions of piety or devotion. In fact, if we begin to measure the fitness of a man for Holy Orders by his devotional fervor or piety, we might mistake enthusiastic religious grammar for the presence of a vocation. Instead, we look to the foundation to see if ministry can be sustained by the human character of this man who desires to "follow me" (Matt 4:19). In some cases, a heart awakened to God's own love indicates that a man has only made a good retreat; it needs further discernment if within that received love of God lays a vocation to Holy Orders.

However, with all that is affirmed about the presence of a sound human character in men who inquire into diaconate formation, it is the spiritual life that occupies the heart of all formation in Holy Orders. Nevertheless, human formation and spiritual communion with the Trinity are not separated in any way. *It is love of the Trinity that humanizes.*[1] One can make a distinction between the two, however, in order to isolate and identify specific character traits that need to be set in relation to a man's communion with God. Men who are attracted to the diaconate must be men who *desire* to encounter the Lord, who *receive* his love as their way of being, and who *carry* his capacity to listen for pain in the human heart all the while knowing where relief for that pain is found within the church. The deacon is, first and foremost, a man of interiority; a man who wants to be affected by trinitarian love. He can assist the needy *as one in Holy Orders* if and only if this assistance flows from his inherent intimacy with Christ the Servant. Anything less is simply ethical behavior or acts of humanitarian charity. Such acts do not need to flow from the supernatural action of the paschal mystery and therefore do not call for ordination. To be a humanitarian is to have a heightened gift of empathy that flows over into compassion for one's fellow man. Empathy is a necessary foundation for assisting others in pain, but it alone does not exhaust the mystery of ordination. And as such, empathy will only remain and deepen over the many decades of ecclesial service if that empathy is sourced in Christ and restored in him when human strength, interest, and generosity lag.

To be attracted to the diaconate is by its very nature to be attracted to the actions of Christ as Servant, and even more mysterious, it is to be attracted to these actions as a place within which to dwell with him (see John 1:38; 15:4). To discern a diaconal vocation is to distinguish between the attraction to "help out" around the parish and the weighty invitation from Christ: "Will you allow me to live my servant mysteries over again in your own flesh?" Does one want to be a man who is *living* Christ's own servant mysteries? This is the central question of discernment.

As the Congregation for Catholic Education notes, "The program of the propaedeutic period, usually, should not provide school lessons, but rather meetings for prayer, instructions, moments of reflection and comparison directed toward ensuring the objective nature of the vocational discernment, according to a well-structured plan."[2] The first introduction to diaconal life is an introduction to interiority, contemplation, and reflection. This matrix is crucial for securing future deacons who have suffered the coming of Christ at new levels of intimacy. They become men no longer able to "hide" from Christ by reducing themselves to their successful secular resumes and competencies. Diaconal spiritual formation is not to be seen as an addendum. Having men learn the ways of interiority with a spiritual director is the only way to have them welcome or deepen Christ's cohabitation in their hearts. The U.S. bishops are clear in this matter: "Deacons are obligated to give priority to the spiritual life and to live their *diakonia* with generosity" (Directory, 63).[3] They state further, "A man should not be admitted to diaconal formation unless it is demonstrated that he is already living a life of mature Christian spirituality....To attain an interior spiritual maturity requires an intense sacramental and prayer life" (111–12).

Such an "intense prayer life" may at first seem to be simply the concern of the man and his spiritual director. However, this is a too narrow view of spiritual formation and the ministry that flows from such. If an aspirant or candidate can only talk to his spiritual director about prayer and intimacy with God, then the spiritual life is defined not simply as personal, but more strictly as private. This militates against future deacons being able to share their own faith with others and discuss the spiritual lives of those whom they serve with a needed level of familiarity and comfort. Without a competency for speaking in public about how the Trinity is loving him, a man loses contact with the vocabulary of interiority. He then "refers" to others, who are experts, all spiritual questions that some may have for him. It is granted that diaconal formation does not provide the needed training to become an expert in spiritual direction. Such training is absolutely necessary for anyone who endeavors to guide another's heart to deeper union with God. For those in diaconal formation, such training in spiritual direction can be engaged after ordination. The diaconal candidate, however, does need to be trained in *how to pray with others*. When doing so he will be called upon to speak about the reality of interiority. He does not need to share anything of a private nature from his own prayer or probe into such with those with whom he is praying, but the fruit of his "intense" prayer life has to be part of the nourishment a deacon brings to others. This would be very similar to how a happily married man does not need to discuss the intimate details of his love for this wife, but he must be able to give witness to how much and why he loves her in both word and behavior. This edifies all and communicates hope to other married couples; the same witness is needed for one's love of God.

Becoming a man of prayer is crucial for good discernment. One cannot say "God is calling me" if one has no knowledge of the affective movements of his own heart. If a man is to become a deacon, his formation actually begins with his own guided discernment. In so doing, he already becomes a man of the spirit. The whole aim of diaconal discernment is to assist men to remove what hinders cooperation with the Holy Spirit, and to cultivate the virtues that are most favorable to His inspirations. The sum of diaconal discernment consists in noticing and yielding to only the movements of the Spirit in the soul. This noticing is assisted by prayer, spiritual reading, sacraments, the practice of virtues, and conversation with spiritual leaders.

God is already removing some of the hindrances to listening to the Spirit by way of an inquirer's own prayer life and his habits of repentance. The largest obstacle to knowing the will of God is our personal sin. Those in formation are encouraged to frequent confession and spiritual direction during this time of discernment. Feelings of attraction toward the diaconal vocation must be discerned; not immediately confirmed. God seeks a cooperative will. Desire is vital to following through on a vocation, but every desire has to be discerned in order to uncover the presence of a call within desire. Without good discernment, such desires may simply be a passing mood or even a neurotic coping mechanism (e.g., "I need to be a cleric to get attention"). Desire draws a man to his future, but the desire itself must carry consolations that are inhabited by God. We know it is so inhabited when peace fills our souls and leads us to acts of charity, a more sure faith, and a deeper trust based upon hope in the promises of God.

In the beginning of discernment, some report that they cannot "hear" God's voice. This may be due to the fact that one cultivated the meaning of daily life with little or no reference to God. The more the meaning of life becomes centered upon God, the clearer his voice becomes. In order for a man to clearly recognize God's voice and not simply respond to his own unhealed needs, it is good to have him develop a deeper prayer life before considering him for aspirancy.

Furthermore, the discernment process is to help an aspirant identify whether or not the diaconate is a way of contentment and sustained happiness for him. How does he see this practically? This question is crucial so that the aspirant can separate any fantasy he has about diaconate from reality. This fantasy may yield consoling thoughts but they emanate from a false reality (ego, unhealed emotional wounds, etc.). Consequently, Holy Orders cannot fulfill such a man because its end does not serve the fantasy. On the other hand, when a man's description of his future life as a deacon squares with doctrine and ecclesial pastoral experience, then such consolation could be one sign that God is calling him to Orders.

In conversations with each aspirant we do not look for academic descriptions of Christ but for affectively charged convictions of how Christ is defining this man. These affectively charged experiences, however, are interpretively held within the sobriety of ecclesial doctrine, liturgy, and community.

We can further help remove hindrances to the Spirit by inviting the man to explore his daily habits. What activities does he engage in regularly that are diversions from the spiritual life—habits of escaping the Spirit rather than letting the Spirit confront and name the truth about the self? A man who is consumed by distractions will be of little help to parishioners who look to clergy to guide them out of a consumerist, materialist, and experientialist culture. The deacon is to be with the people of the diocese as an agent of spiritual renewal and charity, not simply as "one of the boys." In early conversations with aspirants, we are looking for any resistance to interiority: does he simply want to be in fellowship with other men, does he simply want to "belong" to some group, or does he simply want to increase a low self-esteem by aligning himself with a respectful state in life? Does he have the courage to undergo the pain of self-examination into which Christ leads men (see Eph 4:20) so they can be free to serve the Word, preside at sacraments, and inhabit charity? The Church needs *spiritual leaders* who can preside at the liturgy of charity, who can minister the mysteries of Christ and relate these to the secular character of lay life. Only a man of interiority and self-possession, one not aligned with the culture of distraction, can so serve.

Over the course of several conversations with an inquirer, is there a growing sense that he is receiving the vocation with a spiritual understanding? Does he get it? Is he appropriating the truth within his attraction to diaconate that it is not his idea; it is a response to the person of Christ? Is he *eager* to undergo the purification of formation? Correct discernment of our vocation is crucial because it must be cemented at a very deep level of interiority, an interiority born of communion with Christ speaking these words, "Follow me" (Matt 4:19). If the man has only an anemic sense of this interiority, he will be shaken when the crosses of his vocation are laid upon him, and he will begin to have second thoughts, "Did I make a mistake in becoming a deacon?"

We linger on spirituality, interiority, and discernment because of what we know of Satan. He wants to keep our sins, our fears, our rationalizations, our temptations secret. The temptation is to become a private person, possibly one who withholds the truth from himself and God. If we keep these realities secret, then our ministries will be enslaved to them and we will have no freedom and be unable to facilitate freedom to others. We are invited by the Spirit, then, to gently lead an aspirant to name the reality within which he lives. He is asked to name his mixed motives for wanting to become a deacon, to sift through the weeds and wheat. We are asking him to "come clean" so that the vocation, if he has one, can be built upon a foundation of truth. This foundation is secure because the Spirit shores it up with authentic consolations and strengthens it with affective purification, but only in light of one speaking truth. No one comes to ordination without lingering difficulties, but no one should come to ordination unable to name these, own these, and offer these for healing and forgiveness.

Does he understand the role that his wife and family play in keeping him from becoming a "private" person? This role depends upon the level of trust the man has in his family and whether he receives criticism from them with humility. Furthermore, does he have at the least the beginnings of a good relationship with his pastor? To become a cleric, one is formed in a matrix of relationships attracting a man to live in the light, to speak the truth, and not to manipulate or try to take what only God can give: a vocation. The formation team is charged with challenging a man not to live in isolation, not to live with "his own plans" in "his own way." To be inaccessible to others may mean that he is inaccessible to God—he wants everyone to stay away from his secrets.

Finally, to welcome a man into discernment is to welcome a man into the crucible of intimacy with the Divine. Emphasizing the need to develop an authentic and lively interior life is a way to ensure that a man's pastoral desire and competency is anchored in communion with Christ. This crucible is the real formator, and one ought not to be too quick to move men on to the so-called practical aspects of formation. Sometimes skills in practical service can be rather easily acquired, but a man with real spiritual problems can hide these within such skills for years. After all, he is so good at assisting at Mass, good at baptizing, and good at teaching. All this "excellence" can mask an alienation from the self, from others, and from God, and therefore the man of "excellence" can actually be a "clanging cymbal" (1 Cor 13:1). Can the man who wants to aspire to Holy Orders withstand the fire of receiving God's love and live to tell about it? If so, welcome him into the crucible. For the formators, it is their duty to judge whether such receptivity is truly occurring by measuring the change that such fiery divine intimacy ignites in the man.[4]

DISCERNMENT AND THE WAY OF PRAYER

When an inquirer approaches the deacon director to initially discuss his attraction to the diaconate, he is filled with pragmatic questions usually pertaining to time commitment and the depth of study or pastoral training that he will face. He wants to measure the requirements of a "program" against his competencies in the quest to judge his own possible "success." This concern about success and time and competency is normal and quite masculine. Oftentimes, however, the question about time has a feminine source, the aspirant's wife. She is rightly concerned about whether diaconal formation will weaken the bonds of marriage and family. This question about family is crucial in any discernment and needs to be addressed by the individual in light of each man's own marital situation. Many programs encourage or even mandate that wives attend formation in an effort to keep the spousal bond strong. This is good. However, mandating spousal attendance at weekend formation programs or even evening programs can have the unintended effect of automatically attracting only older candidates. Encouraging but not mandating spousal attendance leaves more room for younger couples to come forward and thereby enliven the diaconate in the diocese with not simply the wisdom of age but the vibrancy of youth. We are to take a man's interest in success and both spouses' concern for the quality of their marriage and answer all practical questions up front. In this way the couple or the celibate inquirer can relax, leaving them available to enter the hard part of formation, which is not academics, time away from family, or competency in pastoral ministry; it is rather one's *availability to receive God*. It is commonplace now for ecclesial leaders to admit that the parish is more likely to sacramentalize than evangelize a person—and so it is with the men who apply for diaconate. Many of them are philosophers (men who want to do good) and not theologians (men burned by deep intimacy with the mystery of Christ's own love for them).

As noted above, human formation is crucial in the development of a deacon, but it is so only because it must carry the heavy and sometimes intimidating weight of a *new and healing relationship with Christ*. Many inquirers present themselves as being formed in a spirituality that is more "formal" than personal. The goodwill they harbor and the attraction they notice to Holy Orders can be based upon a lifetime of "good works" around a parish and also a prayer life that gifts them with emotional stability through their dedication to devotions or formal prayers. This way of praying carries with it a certain level of intimacy with the Divine, yet it is one that can be measured as developing rather than attained. It is analogous to a marriage that has settled into a "peaceful routine," even though they could be receiving one another in a more developed dynamic and life-giving *vulnerability*. In this latter relationship, the spouses do not live in a constant stream of "ecstasy," but they do dwell in a communion that is *the center of their imaginations and the source for all their decisions*. The men who enter deacon formation want to suffer the coming of a new imagination where intimacy with Christ is the source and center for all their thinking and decision making. This intimacy is not a level reserved for "mystics," understood in a narrow way as those who experience the rare fruits of intimacy and giftedness with the Divine: imageless prayer, stigmata, levitation, bilocation, visions, and so on. To say that diaconal formation has this understanding of prayerful intimacy as its goal would be irresponsible and perhaps even egocentric as it sought phenomena as an end in themselves. No, diaconal formation in prayer is "terror inducing" not because it will leave men bloodied with the stigmata but because it will leave men bloodied in their struggle to allow God *too close*. A diaconal formation in prayer is a *progressive vulnerability* in welcoming the servant mysteries of Christ as the center of the imagination and the source for all decisions.

What is the way of such prayer? It begins by moving a man who is discerning diaconate into a deeper consciousness of his citizenship in the Church. The men who come to speak to a deacon director about a vocation come "as they are." In other words, they come with a new desire but dwell in the routine habitat of the popular American culture. It has been this culture that formed their consciences, for some, even more so than the Eucharist. The male American mind is political (conservative or liberal), economic (achieve and produce), and hedonistic (relax and pursue entertainment this weekend). Inviting them to consider that our Western ways may not exhaust the range of behavior open to us by the paschal mystery can be a challenge to some men. Part of diaconal formation must be an acknowledgment of how deeply the cult of the political, economic, and entertainment sources have entered the decision-making matrix of the average American male. Therefore, diaconal formation is to assist men in recovering from the culture both affectively and spiritually. To not lead diaconal aspirants and candidates into deeper prayer leaves them, to paraphrase Pope John Paul II, deacons at risk![5] Shallow prayer cannot secure a man's interior life because it only reaches the routine of his behavior, it does not reach the truth of his being: the depth needed to claim him for Christ alone. Without the deepest anchor of intimacy in the Trinity, men will remain stubborn in their interest in this passing world.

To help a man recover from the culture and move Holy Orders to the center of his heart, he needs to expand any narrow concept of reality into a more generous one. This expanded view of reality includes hospitality toward developing an ecclesial imagination; one not beholden to "this age" but one that flows from being set free for freedom (see Gal 5:1). American values such as "achievement" as one's identity;

politicized tolerance; consumerism; engagement with the "new," and endless worries over how to escape boredom drain the soul and place undue energy upon self-consciousness rather than on the pain of others. To become free is not easy for a fifty-year-old man; much patience needs to be employed on the part of those entrusted with diaconal formation. One of the surprising goals of clerical formation in this age is to discover at its conclusion not only a deacon, but a more passionate Catholic. This "surprising" end result of formation is due to the anemic interest many American men have in pursuing an authentic Catholic conscience at the beginning of formation. A typical Catholic man today notices the scent of a *past* religious culture, while being nourished on the *present* irresistible, massive, and nearly universal display of popular cultural and political values.

A key question to ask those interested in the diaconate today is, "Can you teach *as your own* the full range of Catholic moral, social, and dogmatic teaching in an RCIA class?" The pause after that question might indicate to the deacon director that the men who "help out" around the parish may not be living "in the Word" but only visiting it. Without full citizenship in the ecclesial culture, the inquirer will experience suffering during his time in formation. Such formation will introduce him to the truth that what he loves may be the American popular culture and his lifestyle in the same, rather than life and life abundant (see John 10:10). Furthermore, what we truly love is what forms us most deeply. Over the last fifty years there has been some criticism about the quality of deacon homilies, their capacity to bear the catechetical message, and their competency to even pray with others. These weaknesses can only be healed by a radical reorientation in diaconal formation. Deacon formation is not seminary formation on "the cheap." It is not mimicking seminary in miniature. Deacon formation invites a man to enter the mystery of Christ's own radical availability to those in need. It is a formation that enables a man to live in this mystery of availability and be tutored in how to hear human pain and preach the gospel into it (see Luke 10:34). From Christ's own stance toward the pain of others will come the proper objective for diaconal formation and even priestly formation, since the diaconate is a prerequisite for priesthood.[6] Formation fosters the virtues necessary to live in the mystery of Christ's own availability to human need, the endurance to listen until one hears pain, and the competency to pour the content of the gospel into such pain.

To respond positively to Christ's invitation to share in his own compassion, a man must desire the deepest of intimacy with the Trinity and live in the Word, otherwise as a cleric he will be sad: "When he heard this, he was shocked and went away grieving, for he had many possessions" (Mark 10:22). To live in the Word one has to live where the Word lives, and the Word abides in the church. So the first painful movement of formation comes when a man is invited to be uprooted from his former "residence" and see if he wants to live in the church and not simply within the popular culture. The kind of deacon needed today is not a "back-slapping buddy" but a man who has suffered the coming of Christ and lived to tell about it (see Col 3:3). The deacon needed today is one who reaches out to other husbands, dads, or single men to lead them into the spiritual life — a life of *freedom from* the current, the "new," and the now. As the Church lovingly and dangerously teaches, we are only free when we are in communion with the Truth, and the Truth is a Person. Truth has been revealed; it is Jesus. It is not still being searched for by university professors; it is already beheld by the saints among us.

> Truth is not an imposition. Nor is it simply a set of rules. It is a discovery of the One who never fails us; the One whom we can always trust. In seeking truth we come to live by belief because ultimately truth is a person: Jesus Christ. That is why authentic free-

> dom is not an opting out. It is an opting in; nothing
> less than letting go of self and allowing oneself to be
> drawn into Christ's very being for others.[7]

That is what the diaconate is in its essence: the consent by a man to be drawn into Christ's very being for others. What does a man need so that he can allow himself to be so drawn? He needs to learn to listen to the Spirit name what secular sources of his lay formation need to be purified, or let go of completely, so that the Source, who is Christ, can be more intentionally received (see John 4:14). The inquirer can be helped to name his current sources by his noticing how and where he spends most of his time. As noted above under our discussion of human formation, what a man pays attention to identifies the sources of conscience formation he favors. Here we need to challenge the inquirer to pay heed to any resistance to relinquishing deficient objects of attention and to bring this resistance before Christ for insight, freedom, and healing. Furthermore, we need to converse about any resistance in the man's life to scheduled prayer time, spiritual reading, or even attendance at Mass. Sometimes men are attracted to the diaconate and become awakened to a new desire for intimacy with the Trinity, rather than being sent to pursue the diaconate from an already established intimacy. If the man is new to most ways of prayer, especially deeper prayer, he needs to be instructed or even, perhaps, told to wait to pursue a vocation until his prayer life deepens.

On this last point about deep prayer, I want to highlight the necessity of choosing a new way of life within formal spiritual direction. "As she has never failed to do, again today the Church continues to recommend the practice of spiritual direction, not only to all those who wish to follow the Lord up close, but to every Christian who wishes to live responsibly his baptism, that is, the new life in Christ. Everyone, in fact, and in a particular way all those who have received the divine call to a closer following, needs to be supported personally by a sure guide in doctrine and expert in the things of God."[8]

Spiritual direction is the art of listening to the affective movements of a person's heart and assisting this person in relating these movements to the indwelling Trinity. In this way, the spiritual director aids a person to discern which movements are from God—those that deepen faith, hope, and love, leaving sustained peace, consolation, and attraction—and which are simply from the self, or are movements from an evil spirit—those that leave one affectively heavy in relation to things of the faith. For the inquirer, it is essential that he be introduced into spiritual direction to deepen his own self-knowledge and his knowledge of God's desire for his life. There are a limited number of trained spiritual directors today, especially ones who understand the movements of God within a married man attracted to a clerical vocation, so we have to do the best we can to secure adequate direction for the men in formation. This is made even more difficult because the church advises that such men can be directed only by priests. After ordination, of course, a cleric can be directed by any competent person, be they lay, consecrated, or ordained. Since the pool of competent diocesan priest spiritual directors is small, it is helpful if diaconal formation staff engage in conversation with their bishop about the necessity to send priests away to be trained as directors, even perhaps setting one or two men aside to focus upon the spiritual direction of deacon candidates exclusively, especially if the number of men each year is large enough to warrant such assignments. Seminaries all have full-time spiritual directors with parish priest adjuncts assisting them. If the quality of deacons is to continue to rise, we have to consider moving spiritual direction to the center of formation, and for that to occur we need to look at intentionally training clerics to give such direction.[9] Perhaps this would mean that bishops entertain the idea of allowing trained deacons to give spiritual direction to men in formation. As every deacon director knows, it is very difficult to find parish priests who have both the time to give to deacon candidates and the training necessary for such direction.

Here are certain realities to look for when assisting men to participate in good spiritual direction. First, each man must be praying at least a half hour a day. I usually recommend that they do so before the Blessed Sacrament with a Bible present for *lectio divina*. During this time of prayer, which ought to include some brief note taking, a man is acknowledging all the affective movements within his heart (I am lonely, afraid, joyful, worried, etc.). These movements are not simply passing emotions. The man is being asked to listen to the depths of his heart; the place where *affect carries truth*. In this way, for example, a man acknowledges the fear inside him and asks the Lord its origin and what the presence of such fear is revealing about himself and possibly his relation to God and others. In *acknowledging* this movement of fear, a truth is revealed, "I am afraid because I am selfish. If I give myself to God as a deacon, I will have to change my lifestyle." The man then tells God all about this fear in further prayer. For the prayer to be true communication, the man is earnest in his desire to *relate* all the specific details about this fear and self-centeredness. It is the content and fruit of this communication that the man brings to spiritual direction. In doing so he and his director can listen more deeply to God within this truth and *receive* the love that God wants to give to the man. With the reception of God's love, the man becomes free to discern if the fear is a distraction from Satan turning him from his true call to become a deacon or if the fear is a sign of little or no real desire to enter Holy Orders. The inquirer then further responds to God by returning to prayer and keeping his spiritual direction appointments on a regular basis and bringing his notebook so that he can more easily remember the graces that God shared with him during prayer.

Further, the inquirer ought to be diligently reading in the area of prayer, the meaning of the diaconal vocation, and if married, the doctrinal meaning of marriage. Spiritual books on the vocation of celibacy should be read by single candidates, however, married men should also be introduced to the truths of the celibate life in the inquirer stage since celibacy is their vocation should their wives predecease them. The Scriptures should be the prime spiritual reading for men in formation and the fruit of such reading should be ready material for spiritual direction sessions. I would also recommend that the men receive spiritual nourishment from reading the content of the eucharistic liturgy. The Eucharist holds rich biblical and doctrinal truth that can nourish a man's desire to serve at the altar. The men can be invited to read books on the meaning of the lay vocation and also the social doctrine of the church. Besides prayer, the deacon ought to be an expert in the lay vocation and the primary source of lay spiritual-moral living: the social doctrine of the church. In fact, a man's evangelical and intellectual interest, or lack thereof, in these two areas can be a measure of the presence of a diaconal vocation. The actual reading of such books would truly deepen a man's facility with *lectio divina* and clarify if he should approach the diocese to apply to diaconal formation.

Regarding prayer and *lectio divina*, since scripture is the main object of *lectio divina*, one ought to make a habit of reading the Word of God not as "textbook" but as an opportunity for intimacy with the Trinity. In other words, when we pick up the Scriptures we are to listen until we hear. Benedict XVI, along with John Paul II, relativized the importance of the historical critical method being only one approach among others to scripture.[10] After the Second Vatican Council, most study of scripture was confined to a historical approach, with very few professors and students engaging the text with faith as the compass for reason. Now we are encouraged by popes and seminary scripture scholars to use a more generous definition of reason, one which includes the mind receiving the living *Logos* and not simply textual criticism. This movement toward a more generous definition of reason, one not limited to the "scientific method" alone, can only help us form better preachers, men who not only engage the text with knowledge of literary origins, geographical influence, and historical context, but men who are being fashioned and refashioned by the living Word. The living Word dwells in scripture and leads us into conversion and not simply into knowledge of historical origins. As deacon programs form their faculty it would be good to have instructors who also respect this more generous definition of reason and so teach in a way that reverences a more contemplative pedagogy.[11] This kind of scriptural pedagogy can lead to homilies that fill the heart of worshippers with divine encounter, prayer, and not simply data.[12]

DISCERNMENT AND THE LOVE OF HUSBAND AND WIFE

Marital intimacy is the real sharing of the heart and body within the safety and trust of a prayerful and vowed relationship until death. This intimacy is the glue that holds a relationship together. Without it, outside forces can interfere with the commitment and seduce a spouse to look for a false safety elsewhere, an environment where self-donation and revelation will not be secure but, perhaps, only temporarily received—sexual affairs, emotional affairs, immature and lingering emotional dependency upon one's family of origin, and so on. In this temporary "intimacy," a spouse may receive false consolation, mistaking it for vowed security. Much pain is caused by couples who do not bestow intimacy as their primary gift to one another. Intimacy is demanded by the human heart and when real, is its deepest place of rest, and when received within a communion of prayer, becomes the deepest place of life's meaning.

Marital love gives the self for the good of the spouse. This giving, however, is not simply a series of discreet acts of service for the spouse. Love also involves the desire to abide in the presence of another. To live in the physical presence of one's spouse does not mean that union with him or her has been achieved. Union involves not only service, not only sexual intercourse, but, perhaps most especially, the commitment to reveal the heart, to reveal thoughts, feelings, and desires. These heart movements are not revealed in service of the self. In other words, they are not revealed to relieve oneself of an affective burden ("I am angry; I will tell you about it so I feel better"). No, these heart movements are shared because you have come to know that the spouse will receive these interior movements as a sure path to union ("I am angry so I will tell you about it to guard our communion. I do not want this anger to separate us in any way"). Without such deep sharing, a couple may simply coexist in a house, efficiently choosing the most amenable route to accomplish daily duties, but in reality, missing one another, never being in the real presence of the other. To live in the real presence of one's spouse, there needs to be a common commitment to reveal the heart and to receive one's spouse's heart, thus achieving intimacy.

For some wives a possible vocation to the diaconate by their husband is received more as a threat to her spousal identity than a promise. It is an announcement received in fear. Her anxiety is often well-founded, since so many husbands have been "doing and doing" for decades. Now they present to their wife another commitment of "doing," but this one is wrapped in the sacredness of a call from God. How could she stand against God? The answer is quite simple: the wife is *not* standing against God if her husband has refused a life of emotional intimacy with her. God cannot be calling a husband to more when he has not even reached the meaning of marital giving and availability. A wife knows when her husband has received a call because she is ready to "send him." She is ready to send him because the man has been such a good husband that his presence has become internalized in her heart, thereby establishing the marriage in security. This does not mean that the wife holds unilateral decisiveness regarding vocational discernment. Even her answer has to be discerned, since it is possible for a wife to say "no" to her husband's vocation out of selfishness. However, if the marriage has been mature, affectively vulnerable, and based upon the truth that Christ is giving himself as one to the other, then a wife usually sees the diaconate as the next step to an already beautiful story of her husband's presence to her and God's love for them.

For a man to be in his wife's presence does not mean that he gives up all commitments that take him from her physically; that would be an impossible life. To live in one's presence does, in fact, demand a commitment to spend time together physically; but what is most vital is that each spouse suffers the presence of the other as a chosen gift. To suffer the presence of the spouse means that I make choices that *purify* my ego rather than *inflate* it. The mature spouse intends to make choices that carry consoling assurances to the spouse. To console the spouse, we choose to see his or her beauty and allow this beauty to drain out our ego. This displacing of the ego is not easy; that is why marriage is a suffering. It is easy to remain in *one's own* presence. What is life-altering and healing is to suffer the coming of another into the space formerly filled by the ego. If we suffer this coming, we will eventually enjoy marriage, and our spouse's presence. If we keep resisting the death of our ego, or the healing of self-hate, then our situation is clear; our spouse, her presence, and her needs will be seen as a threat. In the case of one filled with pride, the spouse becomes a person who wants only to "take" from you—time, desires, vacation choices, weekend preoccupations, and the like. Or, in the case of the one who suffers from self-hate, he suffers the inability to receive the love of his spouse. "My self-hate pushes away the healing of being loved." In Christ, we can suffer both the death of the ego and learn to receive the love of another. To go through this suffering with Christ can end our "self-made loneliness" in and through his power of love. He will not abandon the couple. He remains always to complete their joy.

Therefore, if a man senses a call to the diaconate, he has to look again at this spousal love. Is he in union with his wife now, or can the union deepen by his looking again at her and acknowledging what he has forgotten about his love for her or what he never fully received from her? She is a beautiful creation of God and a gift to him. Of course, this beauty is difficult to see at all times and in all circumstances; but since marriage is being given to the spouses in grace at every moment from the Bridegroom himself (that is why it is a sacrament), there is always hope that self-donation can come to define the relationship. The cancellation of that hope, from our side, never from God's, is possible if the spouses refuse to turn to Christ and one another for the strength to suffer the death of their own egos or heal self-hate. Only from the *strength* of an affectively and spiritually mature marriage can a man receive an authentic call to the diaconate and have his marriage deepened by this dramatic invitation from Christ: "May I live my servant mysteries over again in your body?"

Even though it is only the man who is ordained, the whole marriage is affected by his "yes" to this invitation from Christ, and so both the man and woman must discern their capacity for generosity. Generosity, however, is not the neurotic choice to be continually active even under the banner of "ministry." The unique contribution to evangelization that the diaconate makes is its witness to "less is more."

The deacon exists so that Christ's own power and glory can show through. In a diaconal ministry that is humble, measured, and contextualized within a whole set of relationships (spousal, paternal, professional, and civic), each man is not called to "take on" a lot of activity. He is, instead, called to discern which activity of Christ he is to gracefully receive within a limited purview. In this way, Christ *maximizes his own glory* and not the man's. In a way, the diaconate is the incarnation of this cultural biblical sneer: "Can anything good come out of Nazareth?" Ironically, the answer is yes—salvation! So it is with the deacon who keeps perspective, gets help for any neurosis to take "power" and "make" things happen, and accept the formation necessary to receive Christ. Like the symbol of Nazareth, the deacon instills no high expectations by his presence within the church and culture, but also like Nazareth he is able to become *a center of surprising influence* through his own restrained sense of self and his deep reliance upon the grace of his ordination.

Surely the deacon is to have initiative but not in a way that is birthed by the cultural value of competition and achievement. Paradoxically, his main initiative is to *receive* Christ's own servant mysteries and exercise them in trust. The essence of living the Catholic spiritual life well is to have the achieving will purified by the receiving heart. All that will be achieved is sourced only in what one is continually receiving from God. The hardest part of spiritual conversion for the western male is to define his new life in Christ as "pure receptivity"[13] rather than frenetic activity. Part of diaconal spiritual formation is facilitating an awakening to the truth that "apart from me you can do nothing" (John 15:5). What makes a married deacon morally possible is his own contemplative receptivity, his own reliance upon grace to effect the outcome of his activity within the church. In a word, what establishes the condition for the very possibility of a married diaconate is embracing *spiritual poverty*. This theme of spiritual poverty will be considered in detail below but for now it must be mentioned as the key to keeping every deacon open to receiving grace from God, love from his wife, and truth from his conscience, compelling him only to prudent ecclesial service.

The Discernment of
Celibacy as Radical Love

A rare vocation is one where a man discerns that Christ is calling him to the diaconate within a celibate vocation.[14] However, as mentioned above, any man who is discerning the call to the permanent diaconate must factor potential celibacy into his own life's commitment if his wife predeceases him. Upon the death of his wife, a deacon is brought into the mysterious eschatological symbol of Christ's spousal identity, giving himself single-heartedly to the church as Bride. He is "brought into" this status by virtue of sharing in Christ's own self-donation upon the cross not simply as a fully initiated Catholic but as a man who has been *further imprinted* with a sacred character. This character renders the man vulnerable in a specific way beyond baptism so that Christ's own servant mysteries can *define* him as his "likeness to Christ."[15]

The sacrament of Holy Orders is the one Christ living his spousal mysteries over again within three different grades of ecclesial service: deacon, priest, and bishop. When these mysteries inhere in a celibate man, they express a call from Christ that possesses the heart in a unique way. Clerical celibacy is a charism/discipline that signifies Christ's own singular fascination with the welfare of his bride, the Church. Celibacy ought not to be reduced to a pragmatic or sociological definition. If celibate life is reduced simply to a way of managing time for a busy "professional," it soon crashes on the rocks of unmet erotic needs. Celibacy only makes sense in light of one being deeply affected by the Person of Christ; so affected, in fact, that the man receives from him *the fulfillment of all desire*. This is why one question for all married men seeking entrance into the permanent diaconate must be: Is Christ enough for you? Do you have or are you going to develop a contemplative prayer life deep enough to satisfy your spiritual-erotic needs for self-transcendence? This is mainly a question about vulnerability before the love of God and one's own capacity for self-knowledge. Those called to the diaconate are answering "yes" to this particular and piercing question: Does the life of the Spirit so fascinate you that you are willing to have the Spirit be the object of your love even without the joy of sexual self-donation to a wife? Here is how Pope John Paul II described such a life in St. Joseph. "Joseph, in obedience to the Spirit, found in the Spirit the source of love, the conjugal love which he experienced as a man. And this love proved to be greater than this "just man" could ever have expected within the limits of his human heart."[16]

Now, a man contemplating the diaconate might say, "A life of continence was fine for St. Joseph, but I would not be able to receive the Spirit in such a deep and satisfying way; I am not a saint." Of course, some discernments are simple, "I am not attracted to the diaconate, no desire, so I quickly can move on with my life." There are other men who are attracted to the diaconate, but then they hear the news of celibacy and pause. "How could I do that for my whole life?" Or for the married discerner, "What if my wife dies suddenly at a younger age; I don't think I could remain single for the rest of my life." I have heard some men say that "the diaconate does not demand celibacy because deacons, unlike priests, aren't busy enough to warrant the just absence of a wife." These comments are most significant. They can be a sign that interest in the diaconate is waning; they can also become the beginning of a deeper appropriation of the diaconate's rich unity with the Episcopacy and priesthood. Celibacy is not "imposed" upon a man because the vocation he is about to enter carries with it demanding time commitments. If celibacy were practical, then many physicians, firemen, and CEO's should rightfully vow celibacy. It is "unfair" for them to be married as these professions "take" them from their families. Religiously motivated celibacy in the Catholic Church, however, is not about the pragmatics of time; it is about a personal call from Christ. If authentic, the call is Christ choosing you, your particular body. Within your body he wishes to live over again his own servant mysteries. This living over again is not simply the result of being baptized; all are called to Holiness by the indwelling of God. No, this "living over again" configures a man to the interior identity of Christ in the particularity of his own servanthood in such a way that the public acts of such a cleric begin from and remain in union with these same servant mysteries. This configuring to Christ's own servant identity is so distinct that it is a *new sacrament* beyond baptism. Jesus Christ defines himself saying, "I am among you as one who serves" (Luke 22:27), and he still is among us as such in the form of the diaconal charism that both fills the church and individual men within the church. It is to this intimate participation in Christ's own servant mysteries that men are called, which gives rise to the possibility that one can be so satisfied in such participation that he finds "in the Spirit [not in a wife] the source of love, the conjugal love which he experienced as a man" (RC 19). For the single man pursuing diaconal life, this embrace of a new kind of loving is immediate. For the married man this embrace may be years away or tomorrow—or may never come. What is vital is the interior disposition of readiness to embrace such a way of loving if one's spouse ought ever to die.

Finally, celibacy has a witness value as well (see Matt 19:12; 22:30). All who are embraced by the beauty of Christ's own mystery within the charism of chaste celibacy witness to the relative values of all earthly goods. This world with all its beauty and goodness is not an end in itself. Rather such value and goodness point to their origin, the source of love in the Trinity. Only God gives complete rest, fulfillment, and satisfaction. Therefore, in the Catholic Church, celibate clergy give witness to this truth: all that is good is from God and in God all my longings are satisfied. Celibacy also encompasses this truth: all that is sacrificed, offered in love to God, is never lost. What is offered to God is in God and will be given from God for all eternity out of his provident will. There will always be a tension in the body regarding this sacrificial gift to God and church. However, the consolation in such a sacrifice is known as one participates with Christ in his own way of living. Such tension ought not to give way to cynicism about the real possibility of one loving God, others, and self in celibacy. For those who can do so, let them live it, and for those who may be called to live it after a spousal death, *prepare* for such a witness in the only way possible: receive the love of the Trinity deeply into your body through contemplative prayer and the true offer of the self in charity toward others. Of course, what is most painfully true regarding some men is that celibacy presents itself as "unattractive" because the primary emphasis in one's sexual life with one's wife may, in fact, be on the self. For this man, celibacy means that "I am losing pleasure," not that I am being taken up in divine love in a new way. Over the course of diaconal discernment and formation, the most fruitful way to prepare for a life of possible celibate loving is to honestly assess whether I *am loving* my wife in marital relations or am I enjoying *the act* that my wife and I are engaged in? Distinguishing between the two is not easy, but it is possible to discern when self-love is present to a real degree. Diaconal formation is a good time to purify this self-interest. Such an emphasis upon losing "my pleasure" can be especially difficult to purify if the couple is still using some form of contraception. Contraception facilitates a disposition of "on demand" satisfaction. Since the whole woman or the whole man is not being given (fertility) nor received, it is easier simply to reduce sex to pleasure "for me." As men we can gauge the level of selfishness in sexual relations by the degree of anger and frustration we experience when our wives say "not today honey."

However, in the event of the death of a wife, the greater pain besides the loss of pleasure "for me" is the sacrifice of having a woman in my life as spouse. Here the true nature of celibacy "for the kingdom" becomes clear. Throughout marriage, the married deacon gave to both his spouse and to ministry but since scripture testifies that "deacons be married only once" (1 Tim 3:12), a new way of loving is welcomed after a spouse's death. This new love enters more fully into *Christ's own way of serving his Bride* — as a single man and from a deep receptivity to the Father's love. To be celibate for the kingdom is not to be lonely. Loneliness stems from personality traits, unhealed affective wounds that repel others, or it is even imposed upon the self by others based upon prejudice or ignorance. Celibacy is not synonymous with loneliness; it is synonymous with communion. "He who is with God is never *less* alone than when he is alone"[17] One can only choose celibacy if one is full of the Other. To be full of God means to abide in a state of affective and spiritual rest because he has entered the spirit and his beauty is received as Truth resulting in interior peace. "[T]he beauty of Truth appears in him, the beauty of God himself who draws us to himself and, at the same time captures us with the wound of Love, the holy passion, *Eros*, that enables us to go forth together, with and in the Church his Bride, to meet the Love who calls us."[18] Celibacy is communion with God, and being with God, one is with the Church. Celibacy for the kingdom is the fullness of communion. This way of living, however, does not prevent one from occasional emotional loneliness, bouts of alienation, neurotic aching for popularity, affectively empty prayer times, or occasional rejections by friends, parishioners, and fellow clergy. It also does not prevent one from experiencing sexual temptation and the desire to hold a woman. Celibacy is a way of *being human*; not a way of avoiding our incarnate state. Anyone who chooses celibacy for reasons other than being captivated by the beauty of God and looking into that beauty as one's chosen pleasure is setting oneself up for disappointment and sadness. Celibacy is not an institutionalized way of consoling loneliness, it is not a default choice for those who have yet to find a spouse, nor is it a "hiding place" for those who carry sexual burdens and attractions. Celibacy is *freedom*. And yet, even in these less than ideal motivations for the celibate life, God can enter and redeem. We need only be open to the goal of celibacy over time: real and substantial fascination with the Holy, so real and substantial that one can be espoused by it!

Notes

1. "We do not replace the evangelistic task by a campaign of 'humanization'. Do we humanize before Christianizing? — If the enterprise succeeds, Christianity will come too late: its place will be taken. And who thinks that Christianity has no humanizing value?" Henri De Lubac, *Paradoxes of Faith* (Ignatius Press, 1987).

2. Congregation for Catholic Education, *Basic Norms for the Formation of Permanent Deacons* (1998), no. 43.

3. See the very helpful multidisciplinary research study on diaconal spirituality by Deacon Ronald Rojas, *Exploring the Spirituality of the Permanent Diaconate in the United States* (Tampa: Aventine Press, 2009).

4. There is a skepticism that spiritual outcomes can be measured, but the Institute for Priestly Formation has successfully measured outcomes in its diocesan seminarian summer program. See Karen Kangas Dwyer and Ed Hogan, "Assessing a Program of Spiritual Formation Using Pre and Post Self-Report Measures," *Theological Education* (Journal of the Association of Theological Schools) 48, no. 1 (Fall 2013): 25–34; and "Assessment of the Summer Program of Spiritual Formation for Diocesan Seminarians: Pre- and Post-Self Report Measures Indicate Significant Change," *Seminary Journal* 14, no. 3 (Winter 2008): 37–41.

5. "It would be wrong to think that ordinary Christians can be content with a shallow prayer that is unable to fill their whole life. Especially in the face of the many trials to which today's world subjects faith, they would be not only mediocre Christians but 'Christians at risk.' They would run the insidious risk of seeing their faith progressively undermined, and would perhaps end up succumbing to the allure of 'substitutes'....It is therefore essential that education

in prayer should become in some way a key-point of all pastoral planning." John Paul II, *Novo Millennio Ineunte* (2001), no. 34.

6. Church law says that the presbyterate is not to be conferred until an interval of at least six months has been observed between the diaconate and presbyterate (c. 1031, §1). The required documents for those to be ordained to the presbyterate include a testimonial that the diaconate was received (c. 1050, §2). It is possible to ordain a man to the presbyterate without his having been previously ordained to the diaconate. Such an ordination would be valid but illicit.

7. Pope Benedict XVI, Address at Saint Joseph's Seminary, Yonkers, New York, April 19, 2008.

8. Benedict XVI, Address to the Faculty of the Teresianum, May 2011.

9. The following is what the U.S. Bishops' document on priestly formation says about spiritual formation: "Since spiritual formation *is the core* that unifies the life of a priest, it stands *at the heart* of seminary life and *is the center* around which all other aspects are integrated." *Program for Priestly Formation*, 5th ed., no. 115. The following is what the U.S. Bishops say about diaconal formation: "[The] spiritual dimension of formation… constitutes the heart and unifying center of every Christian formation….A man should not be admitted to diaconal formation unless it is demonstrated that he is already living a life of mature Christian spirituality….To attain an interior spiritual maturity requires *an intense sacramental and prayer life*." *National Directory for the Formation, Ministry and Life of Permanent Deacons in the U.S.*, nos. 110–12.

10. Pope John Paul II, "Introduction" in Pontifical Biblical Commission, *The Interpretation of the Bible in the Church* (1993) nos. 9 and 14; Pope Benedict XVI, *Verbum Domini* (2010), nos. 32–39.

11. For more expansive meditations on teaching theology in a more contemplative way, see James Keating, *Resting on the Heart of Christ* (Omaha, NE: IPF Publications, 2009), and *Seminary Theology: Teaching in a Contemplative Way* (Omaha, NE: IPF Publications, 2010).

12. See James Keating, "Contemplative Homiletics," *Seminary Journal* 2 (Fall 2010): 63–69.

13. "Prayer is pure receptivity to God's grace, love in action, communion with the Spirit who dwells within us, leading us, through Jesus, in the Church, to our heavenly Father. In the power of his Spirit, Jesus is always present in our hearts, quietly waiting for us to be still with him, to hear his voice, to abide in his love, and to receive 'power from on high,' enabling us to be salt and light for our world." Pope Benedict XVI, World Youth Day, July 20, 2008.

14. See http://www.usccb.org/beliefs-and-teachings/vocations/diaconate/upload/Diaconate_Post-ordination_Report-Web-2013.pdf, 10. About 2% of all deacons in the United States are single, never married.

15. Cf. *National Directory*, 69ff.

16. John Paul II, *Redemptoris Custos* (1989), no. 19.

17. Joseph Ratzinger, *The God of Jesus Christ* (San Francisco: Ignatius, 2008), 80.

18. Joseph Ratzinger, "Message to Communion and Liberation," (August 2000).

2

FORMATION AND ORDINATION

THE PRINCIPLES OF FORMATION

Suffering the Dying of the Ego

The spiritual life is a contest of yielding to a new beauty and jettisoning the attractions that once held the ego riveted and pleased. To jettison these attractions one needs to surrender and entrust one's whole body to the mystery of the Holy Trinity's love, while at the same time enduring the passing of superficial or artificial pleasures that previously held one's interest. One's personal spiritual life is the Exodus in microcosm (see Exod 16:3; 17:3). The exodus to spiritual freedom is a journey through pain and revelation like the pain suffered by one who is engaged to one woman when his "perfect" mate surprisingly appears on the scene. To break off the engagement is painful, but this pain is buffered by the hope of possessing future joy as he entrusts himself wholly to the woman of his dreams. It is the very existence of this dream woman that communicates energy to him, making it possible to sever ties with the reality that previously captivated him. In this situation he is not moving to a future happiness by pure will power, rather he is taken up in the momentum of being called by beauty, holding within it fulfillment. Albeit he is not yet married to the dream woman, her presence is "real" enough that he *risks all and enters a way of trust.*

Analogously, this is what happens to the man who is chosen by Christ. In this choosing, one acknowledges that Christ is real, but then he must contest with all the other attractions that have taken up residence in his imagination and body—realities that no longer seem to captivate, but still have a power in the habits of his history. Christ is drawing but the past is calling. This is why St. Paul called the way of holiness a "battle." We receive grace to move ahead into communion with the Holy Trinity, but only as men who struggle against spiritual forces. These forces wish to keep us bound to immediate artificial consolations (cf. Eph 6:10ff.). To starve the ego one has to recommit oneself to Christ and behold a new object of satisfaction—Christ's mysteries of love. As indicated above, a man cannot move ahead with a spousal relationship if he keeps communicating with his former girlfriend. Saying that the ego *starves* is a good image because letting go of past fascinations and welcoming new ways of receiving meaning and love can be a trying process. The power of vice and its attachments do not diminish immediately. Wounded human nature is always checking to see if it is "missing out" on something, wondering if there is another "satisfaction" to experiment with rather than the one to which a man has committed himself.

As men who are discerning a call to the diaconate, authentic past commitments have already moved one into spiritual maturity, such as all the sacraments of initiation, the sacrament of reconciliation, marriage itself, fatherhood, a growing prayer life, knowing what it takes to hold down a job or advance in a profession, and the virtues needed to maintain friendships. Even with all these experiences, diaconate contains a further and necessary purification: the elimination of any residue of affective and spiritual immaturity. Seeing the diaconate this way may in fact be one of the reasons that Christ is calling a man. To be called to an ecclesial vocation is not a crown placed upon virtues; it is an act of mercy from Christ in light of one's own spiritual weakness. Having mercy upon our weakness, the Lord gifts a man with ordination and all the assistance that such a state in life can bring: the liturgy of the hours, daily or more frequent Mass attendance, service to the needy as ministerial obligation, the responsibility of holding a public place as a spiritual leader, and deterrents to sin such as knowing that one has "to preach on Sunday," or one has to lead others down the path to conversion through the RCIA, adult faith formation, and spiritual counseling, for example. Within all these "helps" and more, Christ begins to slowly shrivel the ego and fill that space with his own servant mysteries. Becoming a deacon is not an honor in the sense that one wins an award for a lifetime of service. In fact, it may be a lifeline of divine mercy to someone who is so weak in the spiritual battle that he needs further and deeper institutional support.

As the ego shrivels and one welcomes the birth of an empathic heart, the aspirant or candidate realizes that this transformation is Christ sharing his own compassion with the man. The one who endures the conversion of clerical formation as his way to holiness receives the new strength that he has needed in order to be received into heaven. The sacrament of Holy Orders is offered as a way to heaven, to holiness. If it is not discerned as such, one ought to never embrace it. The practical reality is that if I am called to Holy Orders, it will be the easier way to holiness for me, not the more difficult way. In other words, the sacrament of Holy Orders is offered to me by Christ as his gift to me. If this gift is received, then Christ will tutor the man in how to accept a new empathic heart and how to make decisions from such a living compassionate center. This type of tutoring is part of the purpose of clerical formation and, most especially, spiritual direction.

To live as one affected by the servant mysteries of Christ, one has to allow Christ full range within the mind, within the imagination. It is mostly the imagination that has to be affected by Christ since the imagination is the reality that stores all symbols, and symbols contain affective power to ignite action. Action is the ultimate goal of discernment; it is that kind of listening that publicly bears charity to the world.

Being Established in a New Imagination

Desire for God directs the mind to behold God in his beauty and to be affected by such contemplation. This contemplation then fires the mind with images—images born of contemplation of the mysteries of Christ as found in worship and scripture. The former useless images and symbols that carried affect and ignited behavior are now dissolved in light of the beauty of Christ. Christ is laboring to unleash within those who worship a new imagination, which St. Paul calls the "mind of Christ" (1 Cor 2:16). Taking on of the mind of Christ is the work of "recovering from the culture" that we meditated upon at the beginning of this book. It is a radical work because it is one that replaces one cult (popular culture) with another cult (the obedience of Christ—John 5:19). Possessing the mind of Christ is a way of participating in Truth. Such participation does not require a sectarian withdrawal from popular culture, but it does require a new discerning presence within this same culture.

In order to cultivate an imagination that welcomes Christ as Truth, a man has to pay attention to the actions of Christ as revealed in scripture. Such attention is necessary because it is only what we pay attention to that enters our consciousness and defines us. The reason a man is now called a "husband," for example, is because his center of attention or imagination has shifted from himself (bachelor) to another (spousal). The more a man pays attention to his wife, the more he *becomes* her husband. This is a man's new reality; he is a husband. To be a husband is now the man's sacramental identity; it is his reality.

He is called now to think, feel, and act out of this identity, and in doing he *stays in reality*. In other words, the man's imagination has shifted from the self to his bride, and in attending to his bride, he actually stays more deeply grounded in reality. By living in reality, the husband actually relates to his wife and not his fantasies. In this way his wife can respond in kind, she can be with him in reality, and since both now live in this new reality they can be in communion. Identifying what we should pay attention to and thus what constitutes the substance of our imagination is determined by our true vocation, the one given to us by God.

What a deacon should pay attention to are the servant mysteries of Christ, and if married, these same mysteries within the context of his own sacrificial vocation as spouse and father.[1] One of the goals of formation is to encourage the men to welcome a new diaconal imagination. The imagination, in this context, is our capacity to stay connected to the truths of faith by bringing to mind the actions of Christ the Servant. If one is ignorant of the mysteries of Christ's servant heart, then one cannot participate in them — either affectively or intellectually. Imagining the servant mysteries, for example, in prayer or when one is reading or even when one is discerning a particular ministry in which to engage, is crucial to the deacon's own growth in holiness. He will not progress in holiness apart from the call of Christ to come and *participate in Christ's own service* to those in need.

As we imagine Christ's own actions in prayer or through *lectio divina*, we are drawn into these same saving; acts. As such, we listen for the Spirit, who particularizes all universal clerical vocations, so that "I" may personally respond to such inspiration in my time and place. To imagine, discern, and then act is to prolong the ministry of Christ in time through one's own faithful action. Once again, this is why a man being ordained with only a *popular* imagination, even one exposed to academic knowledge about Christ, is insufficient. The mission of the church is better served when we ordain men who can imagine new things (see Rev 21:5; Isa 43:19) as the fruit of their being fascinated with Christ's servant mysteries. After due discernment, what springs forth from a deacon's imagination can be better trusted if it has its origin in reality itself: Christ's own actions of service. An imagination that springs from communion with Christ's own love of those in need is not fantasy. Fantasy is born in isolation and pain, whereas sacred imagination is born in communion and trust, such as that which originates in a prayerful vulnerability to revelation. Being possessed by a diaconal imagination assists a man to welcome Christ's own Spirit as Christ is communicating how to best serve charity and truth in the present culture. A deacon wants this life as his own, "I am among you as one who serves" (Luke 22:27; cf. John 13:14–15; Luke 14:15–23; Luke 10:29ff.).[2] This can only occur if the deacon has suffered the coming of the mind of Christ as his new way of imagining ministry. The Christ-centered mind will be his if he pays attention to the sure sources of truth and weans his mind off superficial, transitory, or ideological sources. Once this Christ-centered mind begins to mature, the deacon's ministry of the Word and charity will become attractive within this culture since people are starving for truth. The famished will recognize his words and actions as "true food" (John 6:55).

THE PRINCIPLES OF MINISTRY

The habit of ambition and "success" is so engrained in the American psyche that such values are embedded in the consciousness of men who aspire to diaconal formation. However, these values have their origin more in economic formation than in ecclesial. While economic values—competition—are not necessarily contradictory to the way of holiness, a strong, Christian, anthropological foundation is needed for a man to welcome Christ's own preoccupation with human pain and misery. Rather than "the wealth of success" being the standard for ministry, one might say it is rather the poverty of dependency that is needed to show forth Christ's compassion. This poverty is not material, per se. It is, rather, a psychological, affective, and spiritual poverty. To be spiritually poor is the capacity to endure the pain of receiving love from the Trinity and circulate such love among others. The independent, self-made man cannot receive. Receiving love is painful because such love displaces all our false loves and idols, thus igniting within us the drama of freedom: Do I choose to receive authentic love from God or continue to take artificial consolation in my "own way"? The more we choose to receive the love of God, withstanding the pain of being in his presence, the more God's love will transform us. This transformation dampens our interest in doing things my "own way" and opens up a fascination with contemplating God's ways. In this transformation is the real origin of ministry. Until we embrace the new way of serving by receiving love, we may, in fact, simply be trying to earn God's love or even worse, circumventing God altogether through a life of self-initiated "good deeds."

To receive, one must be emptied. As we withdraw from artificial consolations — such as superficial escapes or even sins — room opens up within our hearts to receive God.[3] God wants to console us, form us, and be the author of our ministries. The primary and most fundamental relationship must be with Christ, who assumed the condition of a slave for love of the Father and humanity. In virtue of ordination, the deacon is truly called to act in conformity with Christ, who lived in continual communion with the Father. Christ's own service flowed from his union with the Father's love and not from any "neediness" on his part to gain influence or be admired. More profoundly, and less obvious, in his service Christ was not looking for more "to do." He was responding to what he was receiving from the Father. His ministry was the result of listening to his Father's love; his ministry was the fruit of receiving and not the result of some mandate to give. Herein lays the fountain of all authentic ministries: his giving was an overflow of receiving the Father's love. Learning to allow such a source of ministry to be our own is the *very reason* for formation.

There is a great mystery to the diaconate that is revealed in the diaconal ordination rite. On the day of ordination little is said about what a deacon should do. Rather, the rite focuses upon who a deacon should become. To become a virtuous man does not seem to be an inviting "work" because there is nothing to see upon its completion; no new ministry, program, or work of charity. Yet, to become a virtuous man is seen to be a centerpiece of diaconal identity and a major plea to the Holy Spirit from the bishop within the ordination prayers. The Prayer of Consecration makes it plain that the Church is not looking for another group of active men—men who do good works; the Church has those in many quarters. Instead, the Church is looking for a group of spiritual leaders—men who live from the inside out, regularly offering their hearts to Christ as places for him to come into and live his mysteries. The deacon must learn to endure this coming of Christ lovingly and, after doing so, witness to the effect that such an interior life has on the larger life of church and society.

Perhaps even more than in the Rite of Priestly Ordination, we see in the diaconal ordination rite the raising of the principle of being over that of doing. Obviously, all those in Holy Orders are ordained to be men who participate in the ministry of Christ, whether bishop, priest, or deacon. All these men are to receive a share in the mystery of Christ. However, from the perspective of believers, the priest is more "useful" than a deacon. The priest can celebrate Mass, hear confessions, and anoint the sick. Of course, a deacon can witness marriage vows, baptize, preach, preside at wakes, funerals, and burial services, and lead liturgical prayers and devotions like the exposition of the Blessed Sacrament, but these are not assessed by the baptized as urgently useful. When a priest arrives, Mass can be celebrated, sins absolved, and sickness consoled or healed sacramentally. The priesthood fills the Catholic imagination. What part of the Catholic imagination is filled by the diaconal mystery?

To be honest, still in its infancy of restoration, the diaconate does not fill the imagination in any expansive way. When a deacon arrives to minister, he does not bring anything so central with him as the capacity to forgive sins or celebrate the eucharistic liturgy. There is a spiritual poverty to being a deacon, for we know that in emergencies even laypeople can baptize, preside at wake services, and more.

When a deacon arrives to minister, what then does he bring? The deacon brings the unique grace of his ordination, a permanent vulnerability to the servant mysteries of Christ. He carries this grace in his being. When a deacon arrives to perform a ministerial duty—baptize, counsel, or pray with others—he is present among the people as one who serves (see Luke 22:27). How? As noted above, he serves primarily by being vulnerable to receive grace himself, being open to the reception of Christ's own servant identity in his heart so that such intimacy may define his presence. The deacon becomes eager to say, "I have to give myself in Christ's own self-gift. The power is Christ's; the cooperation with such power is my gift to him." In the deacon, the Lord desires to be with his people in their need, and the deacon cooperates with this dominical desire by bringing a word of hope to all in the midst of the secular culture of work, health care, law, education, labor, and more. As Christ descends upon the deacon at ordination, he is also descending upon the culture through the diaconal ministry. In this way, Christ continues to wait on the tables of human need through the deacon's receptivity to the paschal mystery. In this cooperation with grace, the deacon extends the presence of Christ so that in and through the sacrament of Holy Orders Christ presides, in time, at the liturgy of charity.[4] The deacon possesses no unique power by virtue of ordination, but he does possess a share in the power of Holy Orders. He also possesses a mission; he is sent by the bishop at ordination as one open to being configured by the servant Christ. This servant chooses to love those in need and, in so doing, assists in evoking the vocation that is theirs by baptism.

Our Western sensibility that highly esteems achievement might say, "Well, that is not much." However, one can say it gets even worse. What a deacon truly brings to any occasion is his own poverty, his own dependency upon God to bear the fruit of his ministry. "I can do all things through him who strengthens me" (Phil 4:13). A deacon sacramentally embodies the scriptural truth that "apart from me you can do nothing" (John 15:5). To be a spiritually poor deacon is to be one who suffers a new desire and new habits. The new desire is one that longs for an interior vulnerability to Christ's servant mysteries (see Luke 22:27; John 13:14–15; Luke 14:15–23; Luke 10:29ff.). The new habits are ones that invite a deacon to a life of continual receptivity to the grace of such mysteries. When a deacon arrives at a ministry, this new desire to be vulnerable and his new life of habitual receptivity arrive with him. These two realities identify the man as poor. However, this poverty is his wealth, for without such poverty his ministry would rest upon his own natural wit, strength, or skills. These natural endowments can only minister to a person's pain for so long and then these attributes become exhausted, revealing their inadequacy for the mission of serving the Church. Only the *spiritually poor* deacon will minister with effect until death.

When a man first approaches the diaconal vocation, he normally considers it as a function, a work to be done, a contribution to the needs of the church. To consider and be attracted to function is not wholly wrong; there is service to be rendered. However, as we have learned from the liturgy, the most important "active participation" in ecclesial realities is interior. Only when one is truly open to God acting in him can the activities of a man's body be a source of healing. The deacon is called to let grace take him up into the action of Christ the servant.[5] This "taking" is not a poetic description of a pious wish but the key to effective ministry. To be spiritually poor is the anthem of the deacon, a worship that flows from the liturgy of his ordination and is sustained by his service at the daily eucharistic liturgy. This disposition to poverty secures a deacon's role in the liturgy of charity. We are to become united to the Lord and "provide a space for the action of God."

Further, the meaning of diaconal poverty can be understood within the context of his most singular liturgical role. It is the deacon who, even if in the presence of the Pope, is charged to proclaim the gospel during the eucharistic liturgy. This is his irreplaceable liturgical role and hence a key to his identity and mission: his voice must be one with the gospel. What makes the deacon a spiritual leader in his diocese, and not simply a humanitarian, is his utter dependency upon his sharing in Christ's own mission of being sent from the Father. This dependency is expressed by his fidelity to an ecclesially formed heart under the guidance of the bishop. Each deacon is invited to suffer the indwelling of God's Word as his only word. This is experienced as a suffering because men favor their own opinions over the objective truth that is Christ. It is the deacon's privilege to embrace the poverty of being subsumed in the Word, a spiritual poverty that calls him to listen to the Word and welcome its forming power. Having the Word of God as his only word implies that the deacon is more disposed to be questioned by the Word than to pose questions to the Word. In this way, his presence among believers, and within society, disposes others to question themselves about the ultimate meaning of any secular value.

As the deacon becomes more adept at living a mature interior life, he relishes his time in prayer and comes to recognize the affective movements of his own heart as invitations from the Spirit to attend to the Mystery that now possesses him. It is his own participation in the servant mysteries that gives to his ministry a potency that at first may seem absent. The deacon is *not* a priest. There is no urgency to call a deacon into a crisis as he carries with him no sacramental matter or power to forgive, confect, or heal. This is as it should be since the deacon is the servant and not the master; he is the emissary, not the Lord. He acts *in persona Christi servi*, not *capitis*. And yet, at the same time, Holy Orders is one; Christ cannot be separated. So, in a real way, this quizzical poverty of the diaconate is a power—a power of participation in the self-emptying of Christ. The deacon, moved in a Marian way, says "yes" to the poverty of his station. Such poverty is not imposed upon him; it is offered to him as a way of intimacy with the mystery of Christ's own kenotic disposition. If accepted, this intimacy becomes a further conspiracy between the Spirit and the Church to save sinners.

Diaconal poverty, that gift of total dependence upon the grace of ordination which is concretely a communion with the servant mysteries of Christ, constitutes the core of diaconal ministry. The core of such ministry is the relationship with the Divine. The effects of this relationship constitute the gift a deacon brings to human need whether sacramentally, as in baptism, or simply in praying with others in need. To embrace this diaconal poverty is to embrace the freedom to receive the heart of the gift Christ is sharing with each deacon.

> The primary and most fundamental relationship must be with Christ, who assumed the condition of a slave for love of the Father and mankind. In virtue of ordination the deacon is truly called to act in conformity with Christ the Servant.[6]

And so the man who comes forward to seek ordination has to be a man *readied to be emptied* of self-concern, and instead suffer the coming of a new consciousness. This consciousness is a spiritual one, one that assists a man in noticing the inflow of God's own love in deeper and deeper ways. The deacon is a spiritual leader, but in order to become such, he must first be led into a poverty of spirit. Becoming a spiritual expert is painful, but is the only "useful" expertise for one in Holy Orders. And so in what does Holy Orders consist?

THE SACRED CHARACTER OF HOLY ORDERS

For such a "simple" station in the church's hierarchy, the vocation of the deacon is complex. The complexity arises from the net of relationships in which the deacon finds himself upon ordination, a net that is not to be escaped but embraced. Unfortunately, the intricacy of the relationships of the diaconate can tempt a man to despair as he makes efforts to please all of his constituencies: wife, children, bishop, pastor, employer, parishioners, diocesan officials, fellow deacons, and more. Along with these relationships and the various calls they carry, the deacon also feels pressed to "perform" well in his ministries, which can be various and often emotionally consuming. However, looking at the vocation of deacon from the perspective of what Christ is sharing with him, the deacon can receive clarity on a vital truth: it is not the quantity of acts of service that matter to Christ, but simply one's fidelity to the character of ordination. Excessive activity and neurotic hand-wringing about whether "I am *doing enough* to help others" gives birth only to stress, not holiness.

The key to living the diaconate in a simple yet effective way is found within one's fidelity to the *character* received at ordination. The reception of this character allows the deacon to minister in a profound way by letting Christ do the work. As one meditates upon the meaning of diaconal character, one realizes that it mediates a gift to be received and not simply tasks to be accomplished. If a deacon receives this gift subjectively, the various and complex relationships that make up his life will become a support to him in his ministry and no longer rivals for time and emotional capital.

What is This Gift, the Character of Holy Orders?

> Insofar as it is a grade of holy orders, the diaconate imprints a character and communicates a specific sacramental grace. The diaconal character is the configurative and distinguishing sign indelibly impressed in the soul, which configures the one ordained to Christ, who made himself the deacon or servant of all. It brings with it a specific sacramental grace: a gift for living the new reality wrought by the sacrament. With regard to deacons, 'strengthened by sacramental grace they are dedicated to the People of God, in conjunction with the bishop and his body of priests, in the service (*diakonia*) of the liturgy, of the Gospel and of works of charity.' Just as in all sacraments which imprint character, grace has a permanent virtuality. It flowers again and again in the same measure in which it is received and accepted again and again in faith. The Church further teaches that: By a special sacramental gift, Holy Order confers on the deacon a particular participation in the consecration and mission of Him who became servant of the Father for the redemption of mankind, and inserts him in a new and specific way in the mystery of Christ, of his Church and the salvation of all mankind.[7]

The character received at ordination has been likened to a brand or wound that signifies "ownership." Then Cardinal Ratzinger noted that this wound or brand "calls out to its owner."[8] In this way, the cleric stands in relationship to the one who has placed his brand mark upon him. "From now on, let no one make trouble for me; for I carry the marks of Jesus branded on my body" (Gal 6:17). A further scriptural understanding of character might be summed up in this Pauline teaching: "It is no longer I who live, but it is Christ who lives in me" (Gal 2:20). Here the scripture underscores the interior self-surrender of the cleric. He is the one who eagerly hosts the mystery of Christ's public service of charity as his own, as his new life. One man, called to be priest, makes himself permanently available to the sacrificial mystery of Christ; and another man called to be deacon makes himself permanently available to the servant mystery of Christ.

This servant mystery and this sacrificial mystery coincide at the Eucharist wherein Christ offers his body and blood in sacrifice and also "gives example" of what communion with this sacrifice can do to impel self-effacing service (John 13:12ff.). Guy Mansini, OSB, notes the following about this diaconal character of service:

> The deacon disappears into the action he undertakes at Mass. His service is more purely instrumental, more purely a serving, and if he is an icon of anything, he is an icon of precisely that, self-effacing service. The deacon's function is to keep the circle of charitable receiving and giving turning, both sacramentally and within community.[9]

To become permanently available to Christ is an objective reality imparted upon ordination, but it needs to be ever personally appropriated anew so its grace "flowers again and again in the same measure in which it is received...in faith."[10] A further witness to this diaconal character in scripture is the following: "The greatest among you must become like the youngest, and the leader like one who serves....I am among you as the one who serves" (Luke 22:26–27). This service, however, does not simply originate in a man's feelings of empathy toward those in need. Ordained "service" flows from communion with Christ, particularly as it relates to Christ's capacity to listen to his Father. As the psalmist notes, "Sacrifice and offering you do not desire, but you have given me an open ear" (Ps 40:6).

Obedience is the virtue/gift that orders a man to raptly listen to God out of love. One way to better understand obedience would be to meditate upon the story of Mary's attentiveness to Christ in Luke 10:38–42. It is an attentiveness that carries the desire to give the self. It is a listening unto surrender. The Martha figure in the story is a kind and hospitable woman who is serving but she, unlike Mary, has not chosen the better part. "The better part" indicates a depth of communion with Christ that readies one *to give and serve out of that precise communion*. The deacon's subjective appropriation to live in communion with Christ is his full response to the objective action of Christ within him that happened at ordination. He is called not to the priesthood, not to offer sacrifice, but to *diakonia*, service. To serve faithfully, the deacon needs to hear what God desires. Of course, this listening or obedience is one of the most powerful, if not *the* most powerful, elements of Jesus' own ministry. "I can do nothing on my own....I seek to do not my own will but the will of him who sent me" (John 5:30).

When Christ inflicts the "wound" of diaconal ordination upon a man, it is to make him vulnerable to the mystery of this obedient service. The desire to serve the Father's will defines the heart of Christ. Is the deacon aware that Christ is now speaking to him about this desire, about the love of the Father he wishes to dispense upon his church? Did the deacon allow the wound of ordination to open the ears of his heart so that he could hear the movement of Christ's own Spirit? Does the deacon wish to obey the Spirit so that he doesn't work in vain (see Ps 127:1)?

There are few virtues more necessary to a deacon than the capacity to listen to Christ in prayer within the context of listening to both the bishop and the needs of the diocese. Listening for the needs of the people and then discerning with God what needs can be served by his ministry is a prayer emblematic of the deacon. He, with the bishop, is called to prayerfully imagine approaches to service that do not yet exist in the diocese or approaches that can be better equipped.

The diaconal sacramental character can be summarized as a grace that permanently orders a man toward participation in Christ's own self-giving, as one who came to serve and not be served. This is the crux of the character: the deacon has become permanently open, unceasingly available to the mystery of charitable service as it flows from the life, death, and resurrection of Christ. This participation in the mystery of Christ's own service establishes the deacon, by right, to facilitate the circulation of Christ's own charity in the church and beyond. The deacon is an envoy of the paschal mystery to the laity in the hope of serving them in their mission to transform culture for Christ. In this way, the deacon takes what grace he receives when assisting at the altar and gives it to the laity, and then takes what he receives from the laity (their love, suffering, and hardships) and gives it to the priest. The priest, in turn, then offers it to the Father, in and with the sacrifice of Christ. All of this service by the deacon is accomplished in obedience to the pastoral vision of the bishop.[11] When ministering, the deacon embodies the spiritual discernment of the bishop who has identified or confirmed the needs of the church and the appropriate response his deacons should take to serve these needs.

Diaconal Life that Flows
from This Character

Receiving the gift of Holy Orders, which is in communion with Christ's own pastoral charity, establishes the deacon in freedom. It is not the deacon's "job" to do a lot of "work." It is the deacon's call to stay in a posture of receptivity to the gift Christ gives—communion with his own servant-love. Specifically, Christ is inviting the deacon to be available *in him* to the needs of the diocese; to incarnate the eternal availability of Christ's own heart to the poor (see Luke 22:27). What the Lord asks of the deacon is clear: Will you say "yes" to my sharing my availability *in you* until you die? Will you let me act in you, through you, so that I might call many to the "banquet" (see Luke 14:15–24)? The deacon's call is to be faithful to the character received at ordination so that the people he serves can recognize and come to know Christ. This fidelity is expressed through the unceasing prayer of the deacon within his heart—a conversation that continually places the deacon in a posture of surrender. He does this because he knows that Christ can do more through grace than he—the deacon—can do through action. Christ is the love that bears all things—the deacon must let him![12]

The diaconal ministry involves activity, of course, but the key to living in Holy Orders is for the deacon to let the *holy* order him. In being so ordered, the deacon lets Christ use his natural and acquired gifts as doorways for grace to enter and increase the spiritual potency of his presence to those whom he serves. Allowing the *holy* to order him, the deacon allows for an effective ministry, but not one that depends upon any "bag of tricks" that might have been used in his business or secular career. Here is where some deacons run afoul and become emotionally exhausted or suffer a form of insecurity or self-doubt, asking themselves, "Why aren't people responding to me? I am a successful businessman, a professional. I am effective at my job; why not at my ministry?" The transition that needs to be made is one that takes a man from relying on his pool of natural talents and years of professional experience to becoming a man who relies on the depth of his communion with Christ; one who relies on his permanent availability to the servant identity of Jesus. How does a man come to rely on this depth of communion? In other words, how does one live the character of his ordination?

Participation in the Actions of Christ the Servant

First, this communion is secured by the very actions of the deacon in the course of his *ministry of the Word*. The deacon is given the privilege and right to proclaim the gospel. By virtue of his ordination, only he and the priest can utter the very words of Christ in the midst of liturgy. Here we have a wellspring of intimacy for the deacon and Christ. As the deacon meditates upon the gospel, Christ draws the deacon into his heart. There, in the heart, Christ speaks to the deacon about his own servant heart, sharing with the deacon Jesus' own will for him regarding ministry and service. The gospel becomes a point of securing communion with Christ so that ministry flows from an interior place for the good of the people served. Ministry begins and ends in communion with Christ.

Second, the simple *service around the altar* that assists the priest and keeps the movements of liturgical prayer flowing smoothly becomes a point of secured communion with Christ for the deacon. These movements are so modest that they become effortless over time, thus freeing the heart to be with Christ in the depths of Nazareth. Here in the "hidden" simplicity of what are common or ordinary duties—arranging vessels, placing books, pouring wine, and reading petitions—the deacon intercedes for the people of the diocese, who may find it hard to discover Christ in ordinary daily circumstances, where love may be void, and only duty and suffering are present.

Third, communion with Christ is secured in and through the specific *diocesan ministry* of each deacon. Here, in the myriad ways deacons witness to the paschal mystery in the secular world, the altar is brought to the culture by the grace of Holy Orders. In a way, the deacon continues his ministry at the altar by "enthroning the Word of God" in the matrix of culture. Hopefully, through his diaconal formation, the deacon learned not only how to minister Christ to the people, but also how to prayerfully receive Christ within the depths of his own heart right within ministry itself.

Through these three foundational realities in the deacon's life, he remains available to the "owner" who branded him. Christ calls out to the deacon from within the brand mark; from within the wound that divine love imparted upon him on his ordination day. There is no separation between the mysteries of the altar at which the deacon assists and the effect these mysteries have upon his will and conscience as he embeds himself within culture to serve the laity. This service flows from the deacon's intimacy with the servant love of Christ. This intimacy is the result of Christ's actions upon the deacon and the deacon's subjective openness to Christ at the point of the wound. Unlike a physical wound, this spiritual wound is to remain open so that the deacon can receive from there the love that Christ is pouring out into his soul. By desiring for Christ to configure him to a life of self-emptying, the deacon supports and serves the laity in their call to transform culture along the lines of the eucharistic mystery—that is, to give witness to the love-infused Body of Christ in public.

If it is true that the deacon "presides at the Liturgy of Charity"[13] and the priest, at the Liturgy of the Eucharist, then it is also true that the deacon gives Christ the freedom to pour oil and wine (i.e., divine charity, see Luke 10:34) into the needs of the church as she labors to give witness to the love of Christ in public. In his ministry to the laity, he empties himself of social standing so that Christ can act in him to encourage the Church to give witness. The deacon makes himself available to Christ so that Christ can minister to those who feel the cost of standing up for the gospel. The deacon remains empty with them, depending solely on the power of grace. This emptiness is full because it flows from the sacramental character that defines the deacon and from the mutual participation of both him and the laity at the altar.

If the deacon is faithful to his call in all its complexity, he will be able to encourage the laity to give rise to their greatest gift in this or any age: to become the church in public. This witness flows from the altar, from the sacrificial service of Christ, a reality the church consumes in love at the Eucharist. Fidelity to Holy Orders flows from a communion with Christ that is expressed in two different but complementary directions: priestly sacrifice (priesthood) and service to those who suffer (diaconate), so that in the end, Christ will be all in all (the mission of the laity). Christ brings us all to his Mystery so he can accomplish it in us.[14] Having communion with the sacrifice will compel us to service, not by force but by the singular beauty of the One who has come and loved us to the end. The deacon's sacramental character, if he stays open to its transforming grace, communicates to him a reality that enlivens and purifies his own conscience and will redound to the benefit of the church.

This reality is clear: among the members of the church is a rank of clergy living a lay life so as to give witness to the servant mystery of Christ. This mystery is united to and flows from the altar but also reaches into the very fabric of ordinary life. This reach, by virtue of Holy Orders, touches the culture by way of the gift of a man who remains permanently open at the point of one of Christ's greatest mysteries: the Divine is ordered toward self-forgetfulness, service, self-emptying, and self-effacing charity. It is the deacon who is charged to keep

this facet of the mystery before the church's eyes and heart so
that the laity may know by way of his ministry how close
Christ is to them in their courageous witness to the gospel, and
so that priests may know that their sacrifices for the gospel are
not without fruit. It is a fruit so tangible that he can see it
before his eyes every Sunday as the laity process forward to
the altar with the gifts of bread and wine, symbols of the trans-
formed culture, for which they labor in Christ. Furthermore,
ready to receive these gifts from the laity in order to give them
to the priest is the deacon, the one who facilitates charity, who,
in the Spirit, circulates the divine self-giving by his ministry.
May this divine self-giving, this wound upon the heart of the
deacon, this brand mark of love, always be the site of deepest
intimacy between the deacon and the Lord.

Notes

1. See Michael J. Chaback, *Love Becomes Service* (Chester
Springs, PA: Dufour, 2013), 55ff., for some further insights into marriage and diaconal imagination.

2. The servant mysteries of Christ, as referred to in the scripture above, encapsulate the truth of Jesus' own identity. His incarnation enfleshed God's own concern to bind the miserable wounds of
human beings entrapped by sin so that they could participate fully in
the love between the Son and Father by their being lifted up in the
Holy Spirit.

3. See Iain Matthew, *The Impact of God* (London: Hodder and
Stoughton, 1995), 100ff., on this very important point about making
room for God in our souls.

4. For more on this term *liturgy of charity*, see James Keating,
A Deacon's Retreat (Mahwah, NJ: Paulist Press, 2010), 64ff.

5. Joseph Ratzinger, *The Spirit of the Liturgy* (San Francisco:
Ignatius, 2000), 173.

6. Congregation for Clergy, *Directory on the Life and Ministry of
the Permanent Deacon*, no. 47.

7. Congregation for Clergy, *Directory for the Ministry and Life of Permanent Deacons* (Vatican City: Libreria Editrice Vaticana, 1998), nos. 7 and 46.

8. See David Toups, *Reclaiming Our Priestly Character* (Omaha: IPF Publications, 2008), 82.

9. Father Guy Mansini, OSB, private correspondence with author, June 2010.

10. Congregation for Catholic Education, *Basic Norms for the Formation of Permanent Deacons* (1998), no. 7.

11. Richard Gaillardetz's emphasis on the deacon's relationship to the bishop is crucial here. In practice, many have placed too much of an emphasis upon the parish work of the deacon and thus, his relationship to a pastor. Once ordained to the diaconate, a man is sent forth by Christ in a permanent relationship to the one who oversees the Church. This deacon is called to serve him, the bishop, in his ministry of oversight. Richard Gaillardetz, "On the Theological Integrity of the Diaconate," in O. Cummings et al., ed., *Theology of the Diaconate* (Mahwah, NJ: Paulist Press, 2005), 87ff. I would add that at its spiritual core, ordination establishes a man in a permanent openness to the mysteries of Christ in a public way—that is, as one sent from the bishop.

12. See Hans Urs von Balthasar, *Love Alone Is Credible* (San Francisco: Ignatius Press, 2004), 116.

13. See Keating, *A Deacon's Retreat*, 66–67.

14. Jean Corbon, *The Wellspring of Worship* (San Francisco: Ignatius, 2005), 151.

3

MINISTRY

COMMUNION WITH THE WORD

The Heart of the Deacon

If the permanent diaconate is to continue to mature in its identity, so also is it in its theological meaning. Securing the theological meaning of the diaconate is partly accomplished through theological considerations that prayerfully reflect upon *diakonia* within the context of a unified sacrament of Holy Orders. Further, the dignity of the diaconate is expressed most deeply when it is understood to encompass two great founts: liturgical service and the spiritual and corporal works of mercy, that is, service to the poor. These two founts interpenetrate, even as they exist distinctly in each deacon's life. This distinct but unified existence is vital for the deacon to embrace. The deacon moves from assisting at the liturgy to caring for the needy in a way that invites Christ to configure the deacon to Christ's own servant mysteries. These mysteries, truly Christ's own heart, define the deacon's ecclesial and spiritual life. Christ opens his heart to press its servant mysteries into the heart of the deacon, imbuing the man with a defining sacramental character.

Through ordination, the deacon has become permanently available to receive Christ's servant mysteries, and it is the deacon's privilege to keep this character—this wound—open to receive these mysteries. In this way, he insures that he will never reduce his diaconal service merely to a form of humanitarianism. Diaconal life is not simply a moral response to those in need. Being in sacred orders, the deacon is called by Christ to be a ministering presence, one that carries the grace of Jesus' own diaconal mission (see Matt 23:11; Luke 4:18; 9:13, 23ff.; 10:25, 29ff., 38ff.; 12:35ff.; 22:24–27; 23:39; John 13:1–20).

Noting the two founts—liturgy and mercy—of diaconal identity, one sees clearly that they are the sources of continual intimacy with Christ; they are the weak points in creation—easily penetrated by God—through which Christ reaches his own most effectively. The diaconal vocation is supernatural. In order for a man to be happy within the diaconate, he must steep his sacramental wound or character in the Eucharist by way of assisting at the Mass, and in the radical poverty of Christ by way of service to a broken humanity. He saturates this sacramental wound in grace by remaining open to and desirous of such grace as his way of being. What helps the deacon remain permanently available to Christ's servant mysteries is his commitment to prayerfully receive his ordination as an ongoing event. Such a man is always receiving into his heart, through liturgy and charity, the life of Christ the Servant. The deacon wants Christ to affect him in such a way; he wants to receive so as to be sent.

DRINKING AT THE FOUNTS

It is not easy to remain fascinated with the holy over many decades of exercising faith and ministry. In Western culture, there are daily assaults upon the imagination that tempt it to become anchored in the flux of distractions rather than remain in the stability of Christ's own self-offering through liturgy and mercy. For a deacon to lose his way, to lose his interest in things spiritual, is understandable, but to accept such drifting as inevitable is to mistake sloth for a virtue. As we journey through time into eternal life, even things ecclesial and spiritual can become routinized; such is the curse of original sin and our human weakness. Only those who endure to the end (see Matt 24:13) will see that the possibilities of the resurrection begin here in time and are not wholly situated in the afterlife. Indeed, if one waits to taste heaven after death, one will miss heaven. We are to gain a taste for heaven during our earthly life so that we will want God; and our wanting is met by his desire for us—thus filling us with heaven.

What makes sustained interest in the holy over many decades even possible is our own response to grace as it prods us to "begin again" and "stand again" even after we have sinned. Aids to spiritual living are deeply embedded in the ordinariness of our days. Such is especially true in the cultural west, wherein the sacraments are still accessible with some ease. A deacon needs to participate in the ordinary sacramental life of the church in order to have the extraordinary grace of communion with the Trinity within him. However, in the life of middle-class deacons, the "noonday devil," or sloth, is a constant temptation. This temptation raises the questions: "Is my ministry worthwhile? Do my prayers mean or accomplish anything?" Underneath such temptation is a deeper pain born of a regular struggle with masculine narcissism: "I could just drift away from the diaconate and who would know?" Since the diaconate is a humble station without much fanfare, those who are vulnerable to bouts of depression, self-centeredness, or laziness are more easily aroused by the siren call of sloth: "Hey, look over here. There is something much better than what you are doing now." The temptation is always to go broad, when the divine call is usually a call to go and stay deep. By deep is meant the fastening of our sacramental character to the continual stream of grace that is our participation in the eucharistic liturgy and acts of service. To keep "looking over the fence" at a priest's ministry or the secular nature of the layman's life is to truly miss the gift of the diaconate.

The diaconate is given to a man because he is weak and needs a structured spiritual life; it was not given to him because he possessed natural gifts of leadership or useful ecclesial skills. Since a deacon is weak, he should stay wedded to the path of dependency upon mystery—worship and moral living. This is his secured path to holiness. Such a path is simple and can give birth to disdain, becoming a doorway to temptation to sloth: "I should be *doing more*."

As in marriage, a man can go astray from his wife when he fantasizes that there is a perfect woman for him "out there." He may even fantasize that he deserves such a perfect woman because of all his gifts, fueling the lie that he is wasting his time with this simple woman. "I have got to start living before I die!" he will reason. This attitude of looking beyond instead of within is the trap Satan sets for those who have given up on deepening their prayer life or, in the case of marriage, deepening their reception of the goodness of their wife. To go deep is a suffering; to go broad in fantasy is a pleasure. Such ease and pleasure are the reasons why a cleric can grow weary of the spiritual and ministerial life.

The Way Out of "Weariness"

The foot washing scene at the Last Supper is an expression of the institution of the diaconate by Christ, since it reflects the doctrinal truth of the unity of Holy Orders. There is symmetry between Christ's charge to the Apostles: "*Do this* in remembrance of me" (Luke 22:19) and his other apostolic charge: "*You also should do* as I have done to you" (John 13:14–15). As Cardinal Kasper noted, "We have seen that without *diaconia* there cannot be a Church, because Christ himself is one who serves (Luke 22:27).Therefore, at the Last Supper…he not only established the idea of priesthood, but, in principle, also laid the foundation of the diaconal ministry. By the washing of feet he gave us an example, so that we also do, as he did to us (John 13:15). In these words one can see the foundation of the diaconate."[1]

Acknowledging the origins of the diaconate in the foot-washing humiliation of Christ, John's Gospel highlights two other expressions of diaconal agency found in Luke's Gospel that flow from Christ's own mission. In these actions of Christ, the deacon finds refreshment and strength against any temptation to sloth. The first expression is found within the story of the great feast and the second is read in the story of the Good Samaritan. The truths within these two stories, along with John 13:1ff., carry much weight for diaconal spiritual restoration and a renewed diaconal imagination. We are charged to stay awake and not be overcome by those who conform to this age (see Rom 12:2). Further, Hebrews reminds us that when we are influenced by the passing age and its values, we "must pay greater attention to what we have heard" (Heb 2:1). The way back to sustained intimacy with the Trinity is through attentive listening to the mystery already given and received.

LIVING CHRIST'S WORSHIP AND HEALING

Over the last few decades, there have been deacons who have underemphasized the supernatural and liturgical component of their vocation in the name of "service" or through fear of becoming too "clerical." This was unwise. Without a vigorous spiritual and liturgical identity, the deacon fades into the vast field of humanitarian service, a noble field, but one that does not call for ordination. It is not "good deeds" that orient a deacon's ministry or found its origin, rather, it is Christ who orients and founds Holy Orders and the mission that flows from it. It is Christ who imprints a man with Christ's own servant mysteries—the sacramental character—and it is this character that must be received deeply by the deacon in ministry and prayer. The most accessible portal through which a deacon can remain vulnerable to a deepening of this character is his ministry of assisting at the eucharistic liturgy. During his worship and service at the altar, it is best to place the accent upon what the deacon brings *from* the altar and not necessarily what he brings *to* the altar. Obviously, the deacon is only at the altar because of his ordination. This is what he brings to the altar: a duty to adore what the Father has done for us in Christ in and through the open wound of ordination that renders his very being vulnerable to share in Christ's own servant mysteries. The "work" of diaconal spiritual life is to keep this wound open and learn how to receive grace even while ministering. If such prayerful availability is not suffered, that is, welcomed as a pain that kills the ego, the wound will soon shrivel as he begins dangerously to call his own natural talents "ministry." However, this "shriveling" is a subjective experience as nothing can remove the objective gift of Holy Orders since it is being shared from the Christ-centered mysteries. Again, what the deacon brings to the altar is intimacy with the servant mysteries of Christ. He is a man who is defined by the service of Christ as a result of his "knowing" that Christ's service has become sacrifice. Such "service become sacrifice" expresses the fullness of Holy Orders, that is, when a priest celebrates Mass without a deacon, the *diakonia* of Christ is fully present *in him* and, thus, even though the "fuller sign" of deacon and priest at the altar is visually absent, its reality is always present at every Mass.[2] In this priest, Christ has shared his mystery of "service become sacrifice."

What the deacon *receives* from the altar as he assists the priest and people is the regeneration of this diaconal character. Without service at the altar and his ache for the grace of ordination as his ordinary cry, any service he gives to the church and culture will not flow from the fullness of his identity as a man "ordered toward the holy." In this desire or ache for union with Christ's own servant heart, we see the power — expressed in Luke 14:15ff. — to shape the conscience and imagination of the deacon.

The deacon carries the desire of Christ to seek those who cannot find their way to the wedding feast (see Rev 19:9). The deacon, knowing the truth that God is a missionary and chooses to include in his own happiness those who know only alienation and loneliness, runs from the altar to the secular culture with good news. The news is good because it speaks to the deepest longings of the human being: "God wants to include you in the wedding feast of love; he is looking for you. Come to the feast." Before a deacon can be the envoy of the Lord, he must first receive the good news himself; he must allow the love of God in Christ to affect him in a deep way, maybe even in an embarrassing way. He is to receive an *intimacy* that makes him feel uncomfortable, because it makes him know that the invitation given by the Lord to the alienated and lonely is first given to him. Unless the deacon lives at this mystical level, this experiential level of divine love, he will only *carry* a message instead of *being* one. He becomes a message of love for the culture, if he actively engages the love of Christ as it is shared in the Eucharist, appropriated in spiritual direction, inculcated in prayer, and received in the midst of his ministry. What is primary in the diaconal mission is to embrace the obedience of being sent from God into service, so that those who long for God's Word of love may be brought into the wedding feast of the Lamb.

In the parable of the great feast (Luke 14:15ff.), the deacon is sent by the Lord into the highways and hedgerows with a curious mission: the deacon is to compel the lost and reluctant ones into the feast. This compulsion is one of beauty and not one that is the result of force. The deacon compels people to come to the feast because they "behold," or contemplate, the positive effects that such feasting (Eucharist) has upon a man, and they want to know the source of such beauty. The heart of the deacon is one that attends to the deepest of mysteries in his assisting at the altar. The deacon knows what effects occur when he centers his life upon a regular participation in the revelation of God's love for his people at Calvary, and this love's tenacity through death unto resurrection. Such a cleric feels the power of God's own cry: "I want my house filled" (Luke 14:23), because the deacon has tasted the desire of God for his people in his own conversion and the mercy that defined such a turn. In light of this deep desire of God, what Benedict XVI applied to the professional charitable staff of a bishop resounds even more in the heart of the deacon:

> With regard to the personnel who carry out the Church's charitable activity on the practical level, the essential has already been said: they must not be inspired by ideologies aimed at improving the world, but should rather be guided by the faith which works through love (cf. Gal 5:6). Consequently, more than anything, they must be persons moved by Christ's love, persons whose hearts Christ has conquered with his love, awakening within them a love of neighbor. The criterion inspiring their activity should be Saint Paul's…."The love of Christ compels us" (2 Cor 5:14). The consciousness that, in Christ, God has given himself for us, even unto death, must inspire us to live no longer for ourselves but for him, and, with him, for others. Whoever loves Christ loves the Church, and desires the Church to be increasingly the image and instrument of the love which flows from Christ.[3]

THE DEACON'S STATE IN LIFE

By participating in the mysteries of Christ, the deacon is sent to those who have yet to see the beauty of these mysteries. To deepen what was said at the beginning of this book regarding marriage and celibacy, the deacon lives in the mysteries of Christ's own servant love by allowing Christ to sublate his own marriage into the core Christ-centered spousal identity—"I am among you as one who serves" (Luke 22:27). In this way, the deacon shares in the unity of Holy Orders with bishop and priest, in its radical spousal donation now made manifest in both the deacon's fidelity to his wife and his service to those in need. But this unity is also known in the relativization in value of that same marital love in light of Christ's call to priests and bishops to share in his own chastity as a sign of the wedding feast of the Lamb.

All Christian married couples are called to such diaconal service, holding lightly their love of self and one another, as the needs of children and the poor call out to them. In this humble married stance, the couple knows that their faces alone are not the end of their married love. Only both of them gazing at the face of Christ internally secures their own love for one another and imparts the strength needed for service to others. If celibate, this deacon shares in the unity of Holy Orders with bishop and priest. The celibate deacon reveals the beauty carried by bishops and priests that we were made for God and nothing upon this earth ultimately satisfies. The deacon loves the servant mysteries of Christ and so draws his spiritual life from his sacramental unity with Christ's own love for the lost.

LIVING CHRIST'S OWN CHARITY

From worship, which is a sharing in Christ's own self-offering of love to the Father, the deacon is sent to bring a remedy for the wounds inflicted upon humanity by sin. Like the Good Samaritan (see Luke 10:25ff.), who poured wine and oil into the vulnerable body of the man beaten by robbers, the deacon is to pour the Word of God into the wounded human soul. The deacon carries this Word in his heart by way of his participation in the sacrament of Holy Orders, the Eucharist, and his *lectio* of the Liturgy of the Hours.

The Word can pour out of the deacon as healing because he is inhabited by this Word. The Word, which inhabits him, also forms him to see the poor and receive a heart to listen to them. If the deacon is among us as one who serves (see Luke 22:27), then his usual disposition is one of searching for those in need. Since there cannot be a church without *diakonia*, there cannot be a deacon without a heart attuned to the brokenhearted (see Ps 34:18). A deacon knows when the Word inhabits him, because he becomes attracted to those in pain, those who are at risk of living life only for themselves, and those who are at risk of living life in despair due to the heavy burdens placed upon them by others or the circumstances of life. This attraction to pain is not simply experienced as moral empathy. Rather, it is known within a personal call from Christ that stems from the deacon's intimacy with him at the site of his ordination wound. A deacon seeks those in pain, asking them if he can pour the oil and wine of the gospel directly into their wounds as his mission from Christ; a mission that prepares those estranged from God to be reconciled with him by a priest and to worship him at the altar of sacrifice.

In living Christ's own charity, there is a conspiracy within the heart of the deacon among the grace of ordination, the indwelling Word of God, and the cry of the poor. This triangulation establishes the deacon in sacred compassion. This conspiracy opens the deacon's heart to Christ's Spirit, thus welcoming the Spirit to redefine the deacon's desires into those of the "groaning" Spirit (see Rom 8:26). The groan of the Spirit is the groan of Love. The deacon wants this Spirit in him because it is the very truth that called him to Orders in the first place. Christ asks, "Will you let me live my servant mysteries over again in you?" Wherever the Spirit dwells, so does self-donation. Such self-donation is at first a cross for all deacons, a suffering. Since we are sinners, our initial reaction to God's ways is to resist them. It is not "natural" for us to be self-forgetful in service, and even if there are those who appear eagerly self-giving in their nature, upon further scrutiny it can be found that some, in their self-giving, are really looking to be loved rather than loving. We all need purification in both the *intention* of our actions and in our actions, per se. For God, however, self-donation is his life. Therefore, all Christian formation is ordered toward God's own life of reciprocal self-giving becoming alive in us. For the deacon, this formation culminates in a life of Holy Orders ordered toward holiness. As Pope Benedict XVI states, "The Father and the Son are the movement of pure mutual giving, pure mutual handing over of oneself. In this movement, they are fruitful, and their fruitfulness is their unity….For us men, giving and yielding ourselves up always means the cross. In the world, the trinitarian mystery is translated into a mystery of the cross: it is there that we find the fruitfulness out of which the Holy Spirit comes."[4]

Thus, the deacon in his formation, which builds upon all the other sacraments he lives, is learning to welcome eternal life in and through his faith, hope, and love. He is learning to yield his heart to the Spirit, who is the love between the Father and the Son. The deacon welcomes this self-giving, this love who is a Person, deeper into his heart, until developmentally his desires become the desires, the groans, of God's own love: I have come "not to be served but to serve" (Matt 20:28). In other words, the deacon embodies the ecclesial vocation of *wanting* to assist those in pain from a pure heart (see Matt 5:8), rather than *having* to assist them. Such service becomes the deacon's very identity; a service shared with him by Christ himself: "I am among you as one who serves" (Luke 22:27). The drama of each deacon's life is clear: does he want this kind of Spirit *within* him, defining him? "The Spirit of the Lord is upon me, because he has anointed me to bring good news to the poor" (Luke 4:18).

This form of living, which can be digested in Christ's own words, "I am among you as one who serves," reflects what can only be called the reason of Christ. To serve, to be attracted to the wounds of humanity, to be affected by human pain and need, and to offer healing for such, is what the Christian mind calls "reasonable."[5] To be attracted to what repels many, alleviating the pain of others, is a "reasonable" attraction because it is the *Logos* itself desiring such ministry from the church and her deacons. Such attraction, which carries Christ's truth in it, is not the norm for reasoning in the Western world, but is unleashed within those who inhabit the sacramental world. To be a man who suffers the presence of the poor and receive their burdens in love is so antithetical to what humans choose each day that it is proof for the reality of Christ's Spirit—a reality that affects deep change in the heart. Such a change is the purpose of all diaconal formation. The deacon wants Christ to affect him in such a way; he wants to receive Christ's own freedom to see those whom no one sees, and tend to such pain that others ignore. The deacon wants to be sent from the Heart that is such freedom: Jesus, the servant.

The Most "Unromantic" Vocation: Assisting Those in Spiritual and Material Pain

From afar, service is compelling. We see it in the lives of saints and think, "I want to do that." However, once "inside" service, it can become a burden, a choice that often comes from duty alone, a duty not always filled with eager longing. This is why discernment of a vocation is so vital. As was noted at the outset of this book, one has to carefully discern the call to the diaconate, because such a call is good and is a "light burden" when rightly chosen. The vocation is "easy"; it should be a delight. This joy over embracing an authentic vocation resides in one's heart so that we can carry the crosses that come *within* the vocation. If both the vocation and the ministerial burdens are heavy, a man will despair. From within the delight of a well-chosen vocation, one can carry the crosses of ministry over time, even joyfully. This joy is unleashed as a man progressively abandons himself to the mystery of God's own very being and activity. The divine being is one that seeks communion with all, especially the lost and marginalized. We know this because God's being was revealed in Jesus Christ. "Divine activity now takes on dramatic form when, in Jesus Christ, it is God himself who goes in search of the 'stray sheep,' a suffering and lost humanity."[6]

In diaconal ministry, a service deepened and sustained *by participation in the very actions of Christ* by way of eucharistic communion, a man becomes accomplished in listening for the pain of others. This is so because Christ is sharing his own heart with the deacon, who not only stands in the presence of God, but now becomes united with God through Christ's own body and blood.[7]

Through the grace of participating in the life, death, and resurrection of Christ, a deacon suffers the ways of Christ himself and becomes one who searches for those lost and in pain. This desire to listen for the pain is awakened and sustained by and in the sacramental character that marks every deacon. This character cradles the diaconal heart and remains the man's permanent point of rendezvous with Christ's own diaconal mission. From such an intimate union with Christ's own servant heart, a deacon, if he prays, can come to live as one urged on by the love of Christ (see 2 Cor 5:14). The deacon, in Christ, can say he wants to find and save the lost (see Luke 19:10).

This is not some romantic quest for the stereotypical "poor." The search for such romantic adventure ended in many being "sent home" by Mother Teresa, for example. She could not welcome "curiosity seekers," but only those who truly wanted to "[fall] into the earth and [die]" (John 12:24). One doesn't choose the lost; the lost choose you. In this choice, the Holy Spirit captures your mind and heart and carries you away to the pain that you can best serve as part of Christ's own mission.

The "poor" are not objects we lavish "our" attention upon. They are gifts received into our puny worlds; worlds made safe for our fears and secured by our choices to control who or what influences each day. Those in pain, who are received by a deacon, are given to him out of love by Christ himself. The pain they reveal to the deacon, the way they carry it to him so that it might be healed by Christ, is the cross fashioned especially for this particular deacon. It is a cross fit to facilitate the death of his uniquely possessed self-centeredness. In such a cross there is no romance, but there is the real hope for this deacon to live in the joy of consoling peace; a peace no one can take from him. This peace is secure because it inhabits him in the wake of his own ego receding. Such diminishment of the ego is hastened in the light of his own receptivity to Christ's mission becoming his own.

Notes

1. Cardinal Walter Kasper, "The Deacon Offers an Ecclesiological View of the Present Day Challenges in the Church and Society," Paper given at IDC Study-Conference, Brixen, Italy, October 1997, see also: http://deaconsplace.org/index.php?option= com_content&task=view&id=57, accessed April 2014.

2. The complex beauty of what sacrifice means in time is summarized by St. John Chrysostom wherein he articulates the connection between Christ's sacrifice on Calvary, its memorial in the Eucharist, and its expression as self-forgetful service to the needs of the poor. In heaven, self-giving is the essence of what living is; on earth, in time, self-giving is the crucifixion and, hence, the opening of the heart to heaven, albeit through love as pain. "You honor this altar indeed, because it receives Christ's body....But the poor man, who is himself the body of Christ, you treat with scorn....You can see this altar lying around everywhere, both in streets and in the market places, and you can sacrifice upon it every hour; for on this too is sacrifice performed." *Homily on II Corinthians.* See Gary Anderson, *Charity* (New Haven, CT: Yale, 2013), esp. chapters 2 and 3 for a very rich description of the link between worship and service and the reciprocity of giving between we humans in our poverty and God in his love and mercy.

3. Benedict XVI, *Deus Caritas Est*, Encyclical Letter, December 25, 2005.

4. Joseph Ratzinger, Pope Benedict XVI, *The God of Jesus Christ: Meditations on the Triune God* (San Francisco: Ignatius Press, 2008), 110–11.

5. See Adrian Walker, "Love Alone: Hans Urs von Balthasar as Master of Theological Renewal," in *Love Alone Is Credible: Hans Urs von Balthasar as Interpreter of the Catholic Tradition*, ed. David Schindler (Grand Rapids, MI: Eerdmans, 2008), 23–24, 30–31. "Divine love occupies the place of reason itself."

6. Benedict XVI, *Deus Caritas Est* (2005), no. 12.

7. Ibid., no. 13.

CONCLUSION

As already noted, before a deacon can be the envoy of the Lord, he must first receive the good news himself. He is to receive an intimacy with God that makes him feel uncomfortable, because it makes him know that the love given by the Trinity to the alienated and lonely is first given to him. Unless the deacon lives at this mystical level—this experiential level of divine love—he will only carry a message instead of *being* one.

In order for the diaconate to be internalized in the theological imagination of the Church, deacons have to suffer the coming of Christ as charity within their own hearts. This suffering *is* diaconal formation. Once the fruit of this formation sustains diaconal life, the witness of these men will penetrate the consciousness of other clergy and the laity, thus setting up the condition that makes *diakonia* a substantive part of the ecclesial imagination. Some of this formation has already occurred in a deacon candidate's life as he faithfully executed his commitments as son, spouse, father, citizen, professional, and more.

Any resistance to having Christ dwell within our hearts as charity is overcome by receiving truth, love, and healing, which are central to formation in Holy Orders. Such a formation is not mostly academic; this would be a travesty of clerical formation. Rather, the majority of effort expended in diaconal formation ought to be aimed at facilitating a man's participation in a sacred mystery. In other words, formation is the ordering of relationships that facilitates a candidate's becoming weak before divine love and surrendering his total self to the Trinity. This surrender is analogous to a man who becomes possessed by the beauty of a woman and vows to leave the single life, dying to all that is not "for" this woman. In the case of the man in formation, the "woman" is metaphorically God and what his "beauty" elicits is clear: "I am among you as one who serves." Formation in finding this passion is central to Holy Orders, or a man will arrange his ministry around his own needs and the poor will still be alone and without the consolation of Christ. However, such passion is unique. It is not desire unbridled and diffused; a passion arising out of egocentric needs. This passion, rather, is Christ's own and he desires to share it with the men he calls. Each candidate for Holy Orders has to cry out for a share of this passion; he needs to lie on the cathedral floor begging the Spirit for a portion of this passion to heal the needs of others. It is a desire that inheres in the man's heart as discomfort, until it rests, paradoxically, in service. With such an imagination, the deacon becomes capable of creatively discerning which of the corporeal and spiritual works of mercy claim his conscience. Overall, the diaconate, especially in its emerging future of youth and mysticism, will water the church and restore her diaconal imagination as each man earnestly discerns his own reception of these works of mercy. Such skills of discernment will be born not of the "good will" of men who come forward for ordination; rather, it will have its source in a much deeper pool of origin: the mind of Christ as it is received in daily participation in the eucharistic liturgy. Along with this vulnerability before the mystery of human transformation in Christ that is worship, the deacon is always to bring his interior life before his spiritual director. In this conspiracy of worship and spiritual direction is born a discerning heart that can enact the works of mercy to meet real need. He will always remember, however, that the greatest need is for communion with God, which is why the deacon is a sacred minister and not a provider of human social services.

Only the mysticism *of the sacramental life* will renew the diaconal imagination of the whole church and sustain the newly restored diaconate as a visible grade of Holy Orders.

The end of all this renewal is clear: both the men who are ordained and the church that carries Christ's own ministry in its heart witness to the fact that, despite the overwhelming evacuation of religious consciousness from Western culture, the love of many will not grow cold (see Matt 24:12). Instead, the love of many will reignite through the embedded witness of deacons laboring within society as envoys of Christ's kenotic love.[1] Such witnesses need the full support of the Church, especially bishops and priests, for these witnesses also carry a gift to all in Holy Orders: a distinct and visible reminder of what is *living within* each bishop and priest—the sacred character of Christ's own servant mysteries.

May these mysteries come alive again with new force in the life of the Church. Ultimately, the servant mysteries of Christ enter the Church through a graced formation, gifting those who are vulnerable to such formation with hearts "that see" (DCE 31). What these hearts "see" is human need. Such hearts leave no doubt in the ones who suffer that they are gazed upon in love; that God is living and has come to serve them. It is the need for God that is the greatest thirst in the human—and it is Christ as servant who slakes this thirst. May such Christic service be the very core of diaconal life!

Notes

1. The best theological expression of this kenotic mystery to date is found in the research of William Ditewig, "The Kenotic Leadership of Deacons," in *The Deacon Reader*, ed. James Keating (Mahwah, NJ: Paulist Press, 2006), 248–77.